Reimagining Language Instruction

Reimagining Language Instruction

New Approaches to Promoting Equity

Sabina Rak Neugebauer
Emily Phillips Galloway
Christina L. Dobbs

Foreword by Robert T. Jiménez

TEACHERS COLLEGE PRESS
TEACHERS COLLEGE | COLUMBIA UNIVERSITY
NEW YORK AND LONDON

Published by Teachers College Press,® 1234 Amsterdam Avenue, New York, NY 10027

Front cover design by Holly Grundon / BHG Graphics. Cover artwork by Jerusha Saldaña Yáñez.

Library of Congress Cataloging-in-Publication Data is available at loc.gov

ISBN 978-0-8077-6888-4 (paper)
ISBN 978-0-8077-6889-1 (hardcover)
ISBN 978-0-8077-8199-9 (ebook)

Printed on acid-free paper
Manufactured in the United States of America

SRN: Far di ale vos zaynen do ongekumen
un ale vos zaynen dort farblibn
(Translation from the Yiddish): For all those who
came here and all those who stayed behind

Contents

Foreword

Educators have long found themselves at a crossroads when it comes to language and literacy instruction. Decisions about how to teach language, how to support students in accessing new texts and ideas, and which languages to invite in to do that work have longstanding academic, social, and societal consequences and have created tensions and, at times, paralysis or contradiction in teaching practices and school policies. This book addresses these tensions head on by presenting a critical way forward that promotes student growth as well as a more equitable society and does so in ways that are theoretically grounded, empirically researched, practical, and moving.

Remembering my first days in the classroom, I am struck by how critical a resource like this would have been for me professionally and personally. In 1975 I first entered an elementary classroom after recent legislation in Illinois required bilingual instruction for what were then labeled "limited English proficient" students. I still remember a large poster in one classroom stating that our goal was to create fully bilingual and biliterate students in both English and Spanish. As a classroom teacher, I was delighted when a few students mastered conversational English and became biliterate. I was baffled that some students, also conversationally fluent in English, struggled with reading and writing in either language. Our curriculum then consisted of materials designed for second language learners (English for speakers of other languages). The emphasis was on oral language proficiency. We also had the grade-level basal reading materials designed for use with English speaking students. None of these materials were designed for our students, and we did not receive professional learning support for how to modify this curriculum or how to teach these materials. In line with the emphasis on transitioning students from their native language to the language of the classroom (i.e., English), we did receive professional learning concerning language assessment. I remember my frustration and that of my fellow teachers because we wanted to improve our students' literacy using our language assessment data, but we did not receive any support on what instruction would help us promote their success in school. Most teachers today find themselves in classrooms with learners with diverse linguistic resources and experiences, and not just multilingual students, but students who speak a vast array of language varieties and registers. Times have changed, but there remains a struggle to understand the most effective and just way to serve the learners in our classrooms.

Since my early days in the classroom there is growing consensus that high levels of achievement are possible for multilingual students and their peers with deep and vast knowledge of language used in home and community settings but with less experience with the language of school texts. Yet too often these students learn in settings that are not optimal. Indeed, fostering access and achievement for all requires that schools receive sufficient funding and select curriculum designed for multilingual learner (MLL) students and their peers; teachers obtain the requisite professional learning and implement high-quality instruction, and there is a schoolwide focus on the strengths and needs of these young people (Carter and Chatfield, 1986; August, & Shanahan, 2006; Genesee et al., 2006).

While what we teach and how we teach it are not the only factors, they are critical components. But more than content and language instructional standards, educators need frameworks—tools for thinking independently and in community with others about what makes language teaching equitable and how to enact this in their own classrooms and schools. Back then I would have benefited enormously from the information and recommendations presented in this book, *Reimagining Language Instruction: New Approaches to Promoting Equity*. In fact, I could have made productive use of this book when I was a pre-service teacher, after I had gained a few years' experience teaching, and in my work collaborating with districts eager to provide a framework for teaching language and literacy for linguistically heterogenous populations on a larger scale.

This long-needed and insightful text takes on school-based tensions around language instruction and does so by changing the lens for thinking about the role and power of different languages in school (Part I), providing critical frameworks and strategies that help educators support language diversity and student performance (Part II), and presenting a roadmap for how to engage in this important work schoolwide. The authors take you on a journey that begins by rightfully arguing that there are multiple varieties of all named languages such as English. The information presented in the first part of this book to debunk conceptions that some languages are better than others is information that would have served as a counterpoint to the messages I received from my own parents. My Mexican-origin father repeatedly asserted that the Spanish spoken in Mexico City was not only correct but also that other varieties were wanting. My mother, a third-generation descendant of Swedish and Norwegian immigrants, pointed to Webster's English Dictionary and the prose found in the Chicago Tribune as the proper language standard for both speaking and writing. These language discourses guided my thinking as I made my best efforts to teach my students. I can only guess that other teachers also depended, and continue to depend, on these ideas about language. The authors push back against such thinking to motivate and center Part II of the book where they provide theoretically informed practical frames for talking about and examining the language used in schools. These include a framework for bolstering linguistic fluidity in school settings and hands-on language awareness inquiry routines that can be used with students to both examine how the language of school texts works and to interrogate the purposes for which this language is often used. In Part III, they provide activities teachers and administrators can engage in that introduce and solidify new thinking concerning language that goes beyond current binaries and controversies schoolwide.

Throughout, the authors have done the hard work of theorizing conundrums such as how to respect and include the languages and dialects of students from non-dominant communities alongside the task of supporting students to become literate using texts that are mostly designed by disciplinary experts and common in schools. One of the ways that the authors achieve these goals is by providing a wide variety of examples derived from their own classroom-based research. These illustrative snapshots into existing classrooms are provocative and insightful, such as the case that includes a Peruvian student who knew several words for the English term, *corn*. This classroom portrait, like many others, provides readers with clear examples of how to build on the knowledge brought by multilingual learners into the classroom and how such knowledge can expand all students' learning as well as that of teachers.

Through these classroom examples that exemplify and reveal the core framework and routines advocated for in the text, the authors powerfully help pre- and in-service teachers understand how language instruction must accompany disciplinary teaching. The authors show teachers multiple ways to teach students the disciplinary language they need for academic purposes and how such language relates to the language students already know. They also illustrate how to support learners in critiquing such language for their own purposes and empowerment. The authors make clear that by itself, their reimagining of language instruction will not change the world. However, their emphasis on collective schoolwide reform—not just individual teacher action—shows how reform can produce achievable outcomes. While teachers can sometimes feel disempowered to change systems that influence how they teach and how their students learn, the authors of this book powerfully suggest that this does not have to be the case. Schools and classrooms can become places where language is taught more equitably and justly, even as we educators continue to contend with, recognize, and work together to transform societal inequality. I would point out that educators constitute a key block of voters and citizens in and of themselves and that they often influence the change many of us not teaching in schools want to promote.

Over the years, I have worked with teachers of multilingual students from rural schools in places like southern Illinois, north Florida, and central Ohio. My experience is that by working with students who bring a diversity of linguistic varieties and seeing the academic and linguistic growth that is achievable in fertile educational spaces, these teachers often become student advocates. In other words, teachers recognize their students' linguistic virtuosity as they make use of and expand their full range of language proficiency. Such a stance can lead to political activity, particularly that which is necessary to provide equitable schooling. The ideas, information, and recommendations found in this book, *Reimagining Language Instruction*, are a way forward for making individuals, classrooms, and schools advocates for equity and for empowering varied linguistic communities in classrooms and beyond them.

—Robert T. Jiménez, Professor Emeritus
Vanderbilt University

August, D., & Shanahan, T. (Eds.). (2006). *Developing literacy in second-language learners: Report of the National Literacy Panel on Language-Minority Children and Youth*. Lawrence Erlbaum.

Carter, T. P., & Chatfield, M. L. (1986). Effective bilingual schools: Implications for policy and practice. *American Journal of Education, 95*(1), 200–232.

Genesee, F., Lindholm-Leary, K., Saunders, W. M., & Christian, D. (Eds.). (2006). *Educating English language learners: A synthesis of research evidence*. Cambridge University Press.

Acknowledgments

It takes a village to write a book that aims to reimagine learning, teaching, and being in schools. This book would not have been possible without multiple groups of people that shaped our thinking about instruction, our perspectives on language, and our understandings of how to share the hard work and experiences of teachers and students. Here we recognize the many communities that helped make this book possible.

To our teacher community: We would like to express our sincere gratitude to the teachers who invited us into their learning communities, told us their stories of triumph and struggle, and included us as partners in their important work of creating welcoming, content-rich, linguistically diverse, and transformative classrooms. This book could not and would not have been written without these inspiring educators. You shared your classroom with us on days that felt bright and easy and on days that were challenging. We feel honored that you trusted us and allowed us to immerse ourselves in these vulnerable spaces. You have taught us so much about what it means to persist daily in supporting students and, ultimately, a better, kinder, and more thoughtful world. Thank you.

To the youth and children: We are indebted to all the youth and children who beckoned us in hallways, classrooms, school libraries, and lunchrooms or toward the cozy corner to listen and hear their stories of joy, loss, fear, humor, and persistence. Across classrooms in different regions of the country you greeted us with openness, honesty, curiosity, and so many jokes. You taught us how much learning is often about seeing the same thing in a new way. Thank you for sharing your ways of seeing the world, and for sharing your snacks, unique handshakes, inside jokes, and smiles while you did it.

To our practitioner-scholar village: This book marinated over years, and the ideas in it required fierce, truthful, delicate, and heavy conversations about the role of language and justice in schools. We would like to say a special thank you to the community of scholars and practitioners that gave invaluable feedback on portions of this book and who pushed our thinking on this critical topic in education. We wish to thank Sarah Engstrom,

Chantal Francois, Amy Heineke, and Patrick Proctor for their thoughtful comments and input on the early drafts of this manuscript. Your thorough, creative, and generous feedback enriched the clarity, quality, and approach of this book and made us better scholars and advocates for justice in the process. We are forever grateful to Elizabeth Blair, Sherry Deckman, and Katie Lambright. You tirelessly reread chapters seen multiple times and allowed us to perseverate on conceptual ideas covered in the book over months while always managing to bring novel, brilliant insights about how to better capture ideas and communicate them in ways that would serve multiple audiences. Thank you for intellectual company as we wrote this book.

To our dear ones: Sabina—I want to express tremendous gratitude to my family, where questions about language and justice originated. I am thankful for my grandparents, Guta and Mayer, who came to this country filled with their stories of love and loss, but without a word of English they struggled to be seen or heard in the United States as the teachers and writers they were in a time before war. To my parents, Eda and Richard, my first teachers, who taught me to strive to make the world a better and more equitable place and showed me infinite love. For Grandma Mary, who taught me early that we all suffer when there is injustice in the world. To Carlos, Sheila, Regis, Terezinha, Waldemar, and Ziggy, for reminding this lover and enthusiast of words that closeness can transcend what can be expressed in language. To Benny, Chano, Fio, Lili, Pat, Romain, Vico, Victor, and Vincent, who taught me that the more languages you know the more humorous and love-filled life can be. To the Marion Anderson family (Hanchien, Meng, and Rebecca) for keeping me grounded, laughing, and well fed on cheddar bunnies during this arduous and at times meandering process. To Katie and Meaghan for reminding me that true friendship can sustain you whether it is up close, from a faraway place, or in the midst of a pandemic. I want to express my appreciation for my sister, Lila, for always being willing to listen and answer a seemingly irrelevant crossword puzzle–like question loosely related to themes in the book (and solving it!) and for always having the right words. I thank Aunt Roda for being the least noisy but most active cheerleader of my accomplishments big and small. I am grateful to Marcio for reminding me daily of the playfulness of language and also the importance of choosing words carefully and believing in my own. Gratitude for Lina: Like your namesake, you are "sunlight," a "garden of fruit," and "tenderness." You provided an important reminder every day that the deep desire to communicate who we are and our own sense of personhood starts so early. Your love of language and linguistic fluidity today is an urgent reminder that we must build the schools we want to see right now, not tomorrow.

Emily—To my parents, Mary Jo and Ken, who inspired my interest in language with their own insatiable curiosity. Mama and Dad, even as I struggled to become a reader and writer, you equipped me with a love of words and with the belief that my own were worth sharing. Thank you. To Junior, Kim, Kenny, Larken, Mandy, Puddin', and Toni, for your words of encouragement and humor, always. To Kevin, for always letting me have the first words in the morning and the last words at night, and encouraging me always. Gratitude to Fiona and Gwennie, I scarcely have the words to describe how much watching you learn and use language brings me joy each day. You have made me a better communicator and teacher and inspired in me a desire to make our classrooms the sorts of places where you, and all children, deserve to learn.

Christina—I would like to thank my family for all their support as I work and live so far away from my beloved Texas. Special thanks to my mom Larinda, who has a bottomless well of creativity that she uses to love all of us in perfectly specific ways. My youngest niece, Lucy, teaches me over and over that language belongs to those who use it to say what they want to say, and Lucy, you are right—you really should write about sharks in get well cards because it will make people smile. My gratitude for them both and for all my nieces is endless. I also want to thank some of my academic loved ones who support me and teach me to grow and to be brave, including Amanda Salinas, Chris Leider, Jennie Weiner, Jessica Tunney, Pamela Mason, and of course, Emily Phillips Galloway. I don't know what I'd do without each of you along this way.

We are so appreciative of the insight and support of all these communities. This book took several years to complete, years that straddled a pandemic, social upheaval, and the total disruption of classrooms as we once knew them. We hope as we emerge from the pandemic of 2020 and are inspired by social movements for justice spreading from small communities to the nation at large, that this book, crafted in collaboration with so many, can support a new vision for teaching and learning.

Reimagining Language Instruction

Introduction

> Wow, when I eat corn it will be different now!
>
> —Arnold, a kindergartener

In an urban kindergarten classroom in the Midwest, eight students who come from diverse backgrounds and speak a variety of languages at home are learning about growth and transformation, with their current unit focused on how plants grow from a seed into a plant. The room is filled with bright colors and is divided into distinct learning spaces. In the front of the room there's a blackboard decorated with charts, posters of favorite books, and the day's schedule. A gray rug in the shape of a half-moon hugs the wall close to the blackboard. Within 3 feet of the rug are multiple tables for five students each, surrounded by pastel-colored chairs. At the very back of the room there are bean bag chairs and a bookshelf, making up what is affectionately referred to as the "cozy corner." Seated on the rug with her students is Ms. Fitz. She guides the conversation from the topic of seeds to other people, animals, or things students might have seen grow and change shape or form. The conversation meanders from an enlarging pregnant hamster to counterexamples of the shrinking of a slowly melting snowperson until only a carrot nose is left or a cookie jar that mysteriously goes from full to half-full, to empty. The teacher encourages these contributions, asking students how something changed, what caused it to change, and in what ways they could observe these animals or things shifting in form.

Ms. Fitz embeds in the conversation questions about language, specifically ways to describe and exchange ideas about change and stages. She draws students' attention to new *vocabulary* like "phases" or "cycles." She is not just teaching her students new words, but also showing them how to link new ideas and concepts together with language that asks them to think and talk about cause and effect (*"First, the seed . . . then, the seed became . . ."*), a *grammar* that emphasizes the idea of change and transformation important to scientific discovery. She has her students watch a video of corn growing over the course of several months and asks them to use language associated with being a scientist by posing questions about what they observe, can document, and conclude about different plant life stages.

These practices, in turn, foster student contributions to a discussion that includes language such as "I notice/I see/I observe . . . and this tells me. . . ." The students learn to attend to functional language that highlights and emphasizes dynamic conceptions of change that can be parsed and dissected using language that signals this specific purpose.

However, Ms. Fitz is not only expanding students' knowledge of one particular way of talking—in this case, by using language associated with scientific discovery. She also asks questions that help her kindergarten students to think critically about how they might talk about these ideas in different ways. She invites students to draw from a diversity of language resources—some learned in her classroom and others learned outside of it—and to attend to the way language signals meaning. Ms. Fitz asks and encourages student questions that promote reflection about the benefits and limits of the scientific terms and language used in her English language–dominant classroom.

An example of this approach is evident in a snapshot from her interaction with Fiorella, a student who emigrated from Cusco, Peru. With students seated in groups at their small tables, Fiorella asks for clarification about the final scene in the video in which the corn is cooked. Unlike her U.S.-born peers, Fiorella comes from a country where there are 55 varieties of corn. She is curious about the type of corn in the video, questioning whether the farmers are eating choclo (the Quechua-derived word for corn that has large kernels and is hefty and starchy) or maíz (a more generic word for corn that can be used for sweet corn, such as the corn most prevalent in the United States). Ms. Fitz, a White woman who grew up in an Irish-speaking household, delights in Fiorella's questions and her use of Quechua to highlight how reliance solely on the English language to communicate information in the school setting can provide useful facts or, as in this case, obfuscate important distinctions, like differences between varieties of corn!

Ms. Fitz celebrates and builds upon this rich linguistic and conceptual addition by asking Fiorella questions about these different words for corn (e.g., "What are the differences between *choclo* and *maíz* in how they look, grow, taste, etc.?"). In so doing, the diversity of terms from Fiorella's outside-of-school experiences furthers her peers' attention to important conceptual distinctions. More importantly, students understand that the word *corn* has been used generically in the video, without any attention to whether it is sweet corn or some other variety, with implications for how it will be used and potentially how it was grown. Ms. Fitz uses this opportunity to discuss how this video, and specifically some of the language in the video, make it harder to identify or notice some crucial information about where and how this corn might grow. She frames Fiorella as a "detective" who uncovered a hidden clue with additional language resources that, in turn, reveal other types of expertise. The idea of being a detective looking for language clues was exciting for all the students. Arnold, Fiorella's classmate, expressed his enthusiasm for these language revelations in his comment: "Wow, when I eat corn, it will be different now!"

LANGUAGE AWARENESS INQUIRY

Ms. Fitz is promoting her students' understanding of the core content she aims to teach (i.e., growth and transformation). At the same time, she is supporting their awareness of language and how language choices and usage influence the way ideas are presented, accessed, and interpreted. Ms. Fitz is committed to teaching language in ways that promote equity in her classroom and beyond. Her practice supports this aim through her consistent use of what we refer to in this book as *language-awareness inquiry routines,* a process of question-asking by teachers and students that draws attention to linguistic features and choices, the role of language in self-expression, and as a tool for exclusion. In this book, we showcase teachers like Ms. Fitz, who consistently use language-awareness inquiry routines to promote linguistic equity. We illustrate how this practice draws students' attention to language features (vocabulary, syntax, and discourse), diverse language resources (e.g., language used for a chat with a pal, a heart-to-heart with a parent in a language other than English, or a class presentation about ladybugs), and language that empowers student voice (e.g., language to support a personal cause or that questions traditional knowledge in school). These routines are iterative and content directed. Attention to language across lessons, topics, and classrooms encourages reflective language choices that allow students to embrace, critique, and challenge the different ways language can be used and interpreted in our world. These inquiry routines highlight how linguistic choices—which words are used, how important ideas are linked by words, and how the language is structured—influence information gathering and meaning-making, and how such choices can include or exclude.

We advocate for the beneficial role of language-awareness inquiry routines because they are aligned with ideas of *linguistic fluidity,* the ability to move seamlessly and consciously between languages mastered in settings students inhabit both in and out of school. This book supports the creation of classrooms that offer this permeability and flexibility. Fiorella's contribution to the discussion about corn demonstrates the learning benefits of linguistically permeable spaces.

We begin with a focus on instruction that supports linguistic fluidity because language use is not neutral. Embedded in experiences with different languages are social judgments about power relations, with some languages afforded more prestige or power than others. We seek to promote an understanding of these entrenched power relationships through language-awareness inquiry that socializes teachers and students to be critical and conscious of how language choices function to preserve or contest these relationships. Language-awareness inquiry routines are not English-specific and do not reflect a linguistic standard. Instead, the equitable language teaching practices supported in this book are intended to instill in teachers and students a critical set of routines, strategies, and principles that support students in drawing from a diverse language toolkit when learning and sharing what they know.

Ms. Fitz's interchange with Fiorella also showcases the role of varied expertise in a school building. Language-awareness inquiry routines usually originate with teacher questions but set off a cascade of interactions between teachers and students that are reflective about the features of language and critical in their ability to highlight how language can empower students. As was the case with Ms. Fitz and Fiorella, it is the back-and-forth exchanges between teachers and students that create authentic spaces for inquiry. Throughout the book, we will showcase language-awareness inquiry routines that educators can use across subject areas, elementary, middle, and high school context, as well as linguistically homogenous and heterogenous student populations. We describe a range of classroom examples from our work developed across content areas, grade levels, and diverse school types and student populations. We present these varied examples to support pedagogical planning and provide principles for supporting impromptu conversations with students at the heart of meaningful classroom exchanges.

CONCEPTIONS THAT PROMOTE EQUITY VERSUS MISCONCEPTIONS THAT LIMIT EQUITY

In our work collaborating with teachers and students in linguistically and demographically diverse schools across the United States, we found that an important precursor to being able to implement these practices and collaborate across school stakeholders successfully was addressing head-on existing conceptions of language and, in some cases, misconceptions about language.

We contrast *conceptions of language that promote equitable language teaching* with *misconceptions that limit* and subsequently devalue language diversity. Rather than solely presenting conceptions that uplift throughout the book, we also attend to misconceptions because they reveal how barriers to equitable language teaching can unintentionally be created. We use misconceptions as springboards for making a case for more equitable practices and approaches, specifically the power of language-awareness inquiry routines for building students' linguistic fluidity, where students can develop the skills and knowledge necessary to move seamlessly and intentionally between a variety of language resources mastered in school and beyond the classroom to communicate one's full meaning. These routines are, at their core, humanizing because they focus on enabling students to bring their entire linguistic repertoire to the classroom in the service of communicating diverse beliefs, ways of knowing, hopes, understandings, and dreams. Throughout, we provide useful classroom case studies for pre-service and in-service teachers and a step-by-step guide for improving instruction, supporting all learners, and taking advantage of all students' linguistic resources to improve their educational journey and their schools more broadly.

* * *

To most effectively promote equitable language teaching and linguistic fluidity, all educators must work with the entire school community—from students and their teachers to administrators and families—to collectively adopt an inquiry approach to language teaching and learning. Inquiry—individual and collective—is a central means of generating knowledge, as well as a critical practice for reimagining new, more just learning spaces (Cochran-Smith & Lytle, 2009). The routines and practices promoted in this book require personal and professional examination of language beliefs and conceptions, classroom practices, and schoolwide structures, systems, and resource allocation that support or inhibit knowledge-building around equitable language instruction. Multilevel inquiry that includes individuals, classrooms, and all school community members is essential for interrupting systems, organizational structures, and interpersonal dynamics that create and reproduce linguistic injustices (Ishimaru et al., 2022).

In recognizing that equitable language teaching must consider these multiple levels, this book is divided into three corresponding parts. The first engages readers in an exploration of *individual* beliefs and understandings of language that can influence the success of language-awareness inquiry routines (Part I). We then focus on *classroom* practices and delve deeper into language-awareness inquiry routines across different subjects, grades, and classroom compositions (Part II). We conclude by addressing collective *schoolwide* language-awareness inquiry and steps as well as processes for supporting teachers in collaborating and administrators in promoting a culture of equitable language teaching (Part III).

This multilevel approach grew from our own experiences as learners, educators, researchers, and teacher educators working in numerous large urban districts. Our cherished and informative collaborations with schools surfaced a growing paralysis around how to teach language standards—particularly those pertaining to "academic language," commonly referred to as the "language of school" or "of the disciplines"—while valuing the rich and diverse language assets students bring to the classroom and unveiling the power relations that entrench school language. We believe this text provides an essential guide to help teachers in both linguistically diverse classrooms and in linguistically homogenous classrooms to move forward by (1) uncovering existing conceptions of language teaching that may undercut instructional equity; (2) examining and tackling the difficult pedagogical charge of recognizing the characteristics of the vocabulary, syntax, and discourse or language that is often expected of school tasks, conveyed in texts and in school discussions while simultaneously valuing, integrating, and empowering students' diverse and distinctive linguistic assets beyond classroom tasks; and (3) encouraging collective exploration into language use by administrators, teachers, and students across the school system and, in turn, exploration into how schools can build a more equitable language environment. This book meets teachers and school stakeholders where they are today to support them and their students in creating and reaching for a more just present and future.

Part I: Individual Inquiry: Dismantling Linguicism

In Part I, we explore teacher and student understandings about the role of language and languages in school. Specifically, we tackle *linguicism,* or linguistic prejudice and discrimination against learners on the basis of the languages they speak and the ways that they speak these languages (Phillipson & Skutnabb-Kangas, 1986). We begin with individual conceptions of language because these often-taken-for-granted assumptions frame how we teach language in classrooms in ways that can be powerful and damaging, and they are often invisible to us. In this section, we promote understandings of language that focus on the value of varied linguistic resources for expressing meaning for specific purposes and for learning and contrast this functional and dynamic conception of language with misconceptions of language that promote language hierarchies. We debunk the interpretation that certain ways of speaking are better, or more "correct" than others, and address how such views create unnecessary pecking orders in classrooms. Instead, we promote a vision of schools as linguistically permeable spaces where instruction focuses on awareness of language features, meaning-making, and power embedded in linguistic choices.

Part II: Classroom Inquiry: Supporting Linguistic Fluidity

Part II of this text more explicitly addresses language-awareness inquiry classroom practices that support linguistic fluidity. We explore routines that focus on language and create linguistically permeable and conscious spaces. To this end, Part II juxtaposes multifaceted conceptions of language with singular misconceptions that see language instruction as about solely teaching vocabulary and "sophisticated" language of the upper grades. This section provides approaches, principles, and strategies for engaging students in discussions that support students' language choices, attention to language features, and a more critical lens for analyzing linguistic power and student agency. We debunk understandings of language as synonymous with vocabulary and address the multiple purposes and features of language that are relevant for instruction at all ages. Even more critical, this section of the book focuses on empowering all students to understand how linguistic choices and resources can support discovery and self-expression across the grade span.

Part III: Collective Inquiry: Forging Communities for Equity

In Part III, we focus on the power of collective inquiry. We consider how schools can investigate language beliefs and practices as a community and build equitable language teaching spaces school wide. We promote a conception of language teaching that includes fostering a new school culture as opposed to misconceptions that focus on teachers as individual change agents. This section provides guidance on how to engage in collective language-awareness inquiry in teacher teams and through structures and processes put in place by administrators to create a more linguistically conscious, critical, and just school culture.

We provide this multilevel, schoolwide approach as a way to highlight specific conceptions and processes that value language diversity and provide promising practices for language teaching, and contrast these with misconceptions that lead to practices that create barriers for many students' learning. We include many examples from teachers' classrooms across grade levels and regions of the United States. As such, this book was truly written in collaboration with teachers and students; the example lessons in subsequent chapters are based on our work with schools, and the insights raised throughout this book reflect teacher input and feedback about how to address the tensions of everyday practice. To protect the anonymity of teachers, students, and schools, we have created composite cases (Creswell, 2018) that combine interactions with multiple participants into one case and/or change identifying details, and all names are pseudonyms. Demographic characteristics of those described reflect self-identifications. We invite you to collaborate with us as you read this book to uncover hidden assumptions about language that interfere with just instruction and to work with us to reimagine school spaces as settings for interrogating language. The instruction that we advocate for in this book creates fertile ground for children and youth to grow, succeed, and be heard.

Chapter Features

This book includes critical chapter features that support the equitable language teaching approaches we advocate for.

First, all chapters include guiding text boxes. Each chapter begins with a text box that includes a key tenet that promotes equitable language teaching. We see these text boxes as useful guideposts that describe the principles that undergird the practices we advocate for in this book. To complement these text boxes on core principles of equitable language instruction, we offer practice-based tips for educators, classrooms, and the broader school community, embedded in the main text of each chapter, to provide explicit direction on how to plan for action and engage in the practices described in each chapter.

Second, each chapter opens with a vignette from a particular classroom and unpacks how a teacher's practice can reveal conceptions of language teaching that limit or promote equitable language teaching or, in some cases, moments where there may be conflicting aims and understandings at work in a teacher's practice and goals.

Third, each chapter includes several classroom snapshots that exemplify equitable language teaching through language-awareness inquiry routines. We include examples that cut across grade span and content area to elucidate how to engage in this iterative, content-directed process of question asking that draws students' attention to the power of language and flexible linguistic choices at their disposal across development and disciplines.

Fourth, each chapter includes both opening and closing reflections. Opening chapter reflections aim to help readers track their developing understanding of key ideas and provide a space for self-reflection about readers' values and goals in teaching students in K–12 settings. Closing reflections provide a space for more in-depth introspection about how language instruction can be taken up in classrooms in more positive and inclusive ways.

And finally, an additional feature of the book is a glossary of key terms. The glossary provides succinct definitions of key concepts that are described in greater detail in the chapters in the book. These definitions are a resource for readers as they move between chapters that cover different but related topics on how to promote equitable language teaching.

* * *

Like Fiorella and her request for more language to describe the nuances of different types of corn, we seek to highlight and recognize meaningful distinctions about language teaching so we can tend to and grow more equitable schools. Before exploring these distinct conceptions and misconceptions of equitable language teaching in depth in this book, we encourage our readers to first reflect on their own understandings, stances, and experiences.

CHAPTER 1 REFLECTION

To begin this journey, pause for a moment and think about your own working understanding of language teaching.

- *How would you define equitable language teaching?*
- *What does it look like, or not look like, in the classroom?*

- *Next, reflect on where you think this working definition, and the images you conjure of what is and is not good language instruction, come from. What experiences led you to define this concept in this way?*
- *Lastly, take a moment to think about how this definition might leave you with some unanswered questions about how to teach the students in your school.*

Part I

INDIVIDUAL INQUIRY: DISMANTLING LINGUICISM

CHAPTER 2

Language Hierarchies Versus Language Resources for Learning

> **CONCEPTIONS THAT PROMOTE EQUITABLE LANGUAGE TEACHING**
>
> Language instruction can replicate existing power structures and the dominance of certain ways of using language; however, language instruction can also work to dismantle these ways by using language inquiry as tools for making systemic oppression, -isms, and discriminatory practices visible, sharpening students' understanding of language choices and their purpose, and encouraging the use of varied language resources.

Ms. Foster-Yu sits with her 1st-grade students in morning meeting in her public school classroom in the southeastern United States. It is 2021 in the midst of a global pandemic and a second-wave civil rights movement in the United States. A central goal for Ms. Foster-Yu this year has been to create a space of hope and to inspire a sense of self-efficacy in her students to address the legacy of racial harms revealed by the George Floyd case and the Black Lives Matter movement. In her majority Black and Latine classroom, the events of the year have been felt by her students personally and collectively. But it is not as if discrimination is only experienced outside of the school. Ms. Foster-Yu is also worried about incidents involving *linguicism* (Phillipson & Skutnabb-Kangas, 1986)—or linguistic prejudice—in her classroom.

Some of her students are speakers of *Black English language* (also called "African American English" or "African American Vernacular English"), some are speakers of languages other than English, and others are not. Recently, when one of her students, Marcus, said, "He be late for the party." Ella, another student who is also Black, was quick to correct him: "'He *is* late for the party,' that's what you should say, Marcus." Later in the week when Yulia, an English learner designated student, spoke in Russian to herself, Julio, a former English learner designated student and Spanish-English speaker, harshly chided her: "This is English only in school! Use good language!" Ms. Foster-Yu felt immediately deflated. As the daughter of Mandarin speaking parents who learned English as adults, watching

Ella and Julio reprimand Marcus and Yulia evoked the painful memory of her own mother experiencing linguistic prejudice. Indeed, she was aware that children often internalize linguistic hierarchies, having done so herself as a child (i.e., standardized English, sometimes called White Mainstream English, mainstream English or dominant English, for example, being viewed as "better" or "correct in relation to other forms of English"). For this reason, she had spent the year trying to create space for all of her students' linguistic resources; however, Ella's and Julio's reactions made her question what she could do differently. Ms. Foster-Yu wondered: *Could she help her students be more linguistically equitable by giving them more language to talk about these ideas?*

Inspired by the class's other morning meeting conversations that were productive, she took a fresh approach with her students the following week:

Ms. Foster-Yu: Do you remember that we talked about racism together last week? Do you remember what that word meant, friends?

Maddie: I think it's about when you're mean to somebody because you don't like their skin's color, so . . . you think one skin color is better.

Marcus: And, I think you need to say that it really hurts people. Like not always on the body, but in the inside you might feel sad.

Maddie: Also, like, maybe you don't get to do things like we talked about the books and the time when the boy could not go to the library.

Ms. Foster-Yu: Right, John Lewis, we talked about how racism hurt him as a child because he could not use the books in the library. In this classroom there are lots of people with different skin colors. And, some people have different religions, or speak different languages and talk in different ways and sometimes those are other reasons that people might treat someone in unkind ways. This is a new word that we can use, it is "prejudice." This word means that somebody doesn't like another person before they even have met them because of their race or religion! Pre- means before, so like in pre-pare (writes on a small white board, underlining root). Prejudice means pre-judging someone. Has anyone ever had this happen to them?

Johannes: Well, I think kids get prejudiced all the time.

Kim Lin: Like, we can't do things? People think we can't do things?

Ms. Foster-Yu: Good example, I think kids do face prejudice. Do you think prejudice is something we need to think about in our classroom? *For example, if one of our friends speaks differently from us, is that okay? What if I spoke Chinese here at school, or spoke English in ways that were different, would that be okay?*

In this example, Ms. Foster-Yu hopes to offer her students new language—and with that, a new concept—to help them to conceptualize the need to view all classmates' language resources as valuable. As the discussion continues in this morning meeting and over the duration of the civil rights unit, Ms. Foster-Yu returns to the concept and language of prejudice. She gradually adds layers until students come to understand that prejudice can manifest not only in how we view others with different skin colors, but also in how we view their language resources. The impact is not only discernable in her students' uptake of the terms she explicitly taught, but also in how they respond to classmates' language resources. Indeed, Ms. Foster-Yu hoped that her students would come to internalize the understanding that "policing" peers' language use was not a helpful practice. She hoped that all members of the classroom community were engaged in listening to understand, which she reinforced through her own active listening to the students' contributions and her modeling of rephrasing ("I think Davio is saying. . . . Is that what you meant, D?"). Before long, her students also engaged in practices that focused on the meaningful exchange of ideas.

Of course, Ms. Foster-Yu is not only teaching new terminology—she is also teaching her students to reflect on language and the elements that comprise it through her morphology-focused lesson on the prefix "pre-": a metalinguistic aim of the lesson. Indeed, understanding the meaning of pre- (before) sets her students up to understand that prejudice often involves judging others before we come to know them as people: a transformational aim of the lesson.

To implement this inquiry approach to language, Ms. Foster-Yu intentionally planned her lesson to focus on both teaching the rich language needed for her students to discuss the various concepts that comprised her unit on civil rights (*metalinguistic* pedagogical aims) *and* to engage in critical evaluation of language hierarchies (*transformational* pedagogical aims). She took an additive approach in which new language is added to students' existing language resources and engaged both the resources they possessed already and those being acquired as they learned. In Figure 2.1 we show some key questions Ms. Foster-Yu prepared for her lesson. These questions emerge from her two aims, both of which are central to equitable language teaching and the effective language-awareness inquiry routines promoted in this book: (1) the instructional study of language and the ability to reflect on language choices and use can make social inequality visible and, as such, can be a powerful practice for empowering students to use their voices (McClain et al., 2021) and (2) pedagogy focused on investigating language should be grounded in the aim of uncovering injustice for the purpose of working toward social transformation (Muhammad, 2020). While language teaching often has metalinguistic aims that can be achieved without a focus on developing students' critical evaluation of linguistic power differentials, we caution that failing to attend to the way language is linked with power can result in teaching that reproduces language hierarchies.

Therefore, metalinguistic and transformational pedagogical aims must work in tandem. Indeed, the language features focused on for instruction should be selected based on transformational aims, that is, as a way of making visible language that is used to include or exclude different communities and for the purpose of equipping students with language that draws attention to power relations (Pennycook, 2001/2021). Even language used in everyday math learning, for example, can function to exclude some students from the community of mathematicians, who have traditionally been male and White across history. This language is used both to make visible mathematical thinking (terms like "proof," "take away," and "derive") and cue certain ways of interacting with the numbers and, when students are unfamiliar with this language, to exclude or alienate (intentionally or unintentionally). Unmasking both the mathematical activity and the historical ways this language has been used to exclude is a transformational aim as it invites students to join the mathematics community and to critique systems that might prevent minoritized students' entry. At the elementary level, in Ms. Foster-Yu's class, for example, she invited students to use all language to express mathematical thinking and included sources that featured people of color and women as STEM innovators (https://www.engineeringforkids.com/about/news/2021/february/10-black-innovators-who-have-made-an-impact-in-s/). This work must continue through the school years to be impactful. This may involve, for example, asking students at the middle and high school levels to engage with newspaper articles and blogs that discuss asymmetric participation in STEM fields (e.g., https://www.pewresearch.org/science/2022/04/07/black-americans-views-of-education-and-professional-opportunities-in-science-technology-engineering-and-math/) and to consider how language and other disciplinary practices may perpetuate exclusion (e.g., https://sites.ed.gov/whblackeducation/files/2016/09/STEM-Fact-Sheet-9.22.16.pdf). Additional language, terms like "unconscious bias" and "systems of oppression," offers language for transformation as they explicitly offer means of talking about often invisible ways students are excluded from societal goods and privilege.

In Figure 2.1 we illustrate Ms. Foster-Yu's planning for her lesson on linguicism, including her two pedagogical aims and some of her prepared prompts to enact these aims.

This chapter explores tensions that arise when seeking to teach language equitably in a society in which *linguicism* is deeply ingrained. Our focus is on divergent conceptions of language teaching that attempt to address linguicism while still teaching the language needed to access content. Often state standards, testing, and curricular resources only serve to re-inscribe views of language as hierarchical, making the work of teaching in ways that view all language resources of equal value particularly challenging. In addition, as illustrated in Ms. Foster-Yu's class, students themselves often bring internalized understandings about language that we must address in order

Figure 2.1. Ms. Foster-Yu's Prepared Aims and Prompts

Questions	Metalinguistic Aim	Transformational Aim
"Pre-" means before, like in pre-pare. Prejudice means pre-judging someone. Has anyone ever had this happen to them?	Word parts can unlock the meaning of unfamiliar words.	Language about linguicism can uncover injustice and defend social change.
What does it mean to "make change" in the way I'm using it now?	Linking words in different ways carries different meaning.	
Why use, "for example"?	Language style and structure supports distinctive ways of defending your stance.	

to create classrooms that are welcoming to all students' linguistic resources (Phillips Galloway et al., 2015; Heineke & Neugebauer, 2018). As Hilary Janks (2000) argues, there is a paradox at play: As we teach the language of school, usually standardized English, we may be simply upholding existing power structures and dominant ways of using language, further increasing their power and dominance; failing to teach this language, however, denies students access to educational and economic opportunity in a society that continues to value academic language skills.

We argue that educators *can* navigate this paradox through equitable language teaching that addresses: the ways in which language teaching has been used historically to perpetuate colonial, racist, and imperialistic agendas; the ways in which language teaching is used as a tool to reify linguistic hierarchies, but also potentially as a resource for supporting text comprehension, written expression, and for questioning linguistic oppression; and, the ways in which language teaching might be reimagined more justly to promote varied language resources in schools and beyond them. We offer two case examples of teachers in elementary and secondary settings who see the varied languages in their classrooms as opportunities to unpack and help students to question language hierarchies using language-awareness inquiry routines.

This chapter emphasizes conceptions of language teaching that promote ways students can be savvy language users, that is, selective in their linguistic choices for academic and other purposes. We also analyze conceptions of language teaching shaped by state standards, state testing, and recent research, that have resulted, in some cases, in unintentionally reifying hierarchies of privilege. Ensuring that language instruction serves all students requires careful and constant vigilance.

CHAPTER 2 REFLECTION

Take a moment to think about your own language hierarchies and the ways that context shapes the language choices that you make each day. Do you place greater value on speaking a certain way with students in school, with colleagues, with your administrator? What does that language look like? What purpose does your language serve?

Now think about your students. How might they answer these questions? Do they place greater value on certain ways of speaking in school, outside of school, or in their communication with friends? How are these hierarchies the same or different?

In this chapter we begin to unpack a misconception of language that limits equitable language teaching, that is, that certain language forms are more privileged or should be more valued than others, and instead aim to promote a conception that promotes equitable language teaching. All languages and ways of talking serve a purpose, and it is the study of those purposes that helps support language teaching, learning, and social transformation. To unpack the misconception that certain language forms should be valued over others, we begin with a discussion of linguicism, arguing that linguicism will continue to be a feature of instruction in the future if we do not begin to address it today. In the sections that follow, we share instructional practices that address historical and present manifestations of linguicism in language instruction.

CONCEPTIONS THAT LIMIT EQUITABLE LANGUAGE INSTRUCTION: LANGUAGE HIERARCHIES

What Is Linguicism?: Unveiling an Often Invisible "-Ism"

In classrooms, we are often aware of the pernicious impacts of racism, sexism, and classism, but less aware of the impact of linguicism. Phillipson and Skutnabb-Kangas (1986) define linguicism as: "ideologies, structures, and practices which are used to legitimate, effectuate, regulate and reproduce an unequal division of power and resources (both material and immaterial) between groups which are defined on the basis of language" (Skutnabb-Kangas, 2015). An important facet of addressing and dismantling linguicism is to recognize that it operates in the very fabric of schooling, both historically and in the present.

Interrogating School Language's Roots, From Settler Colonialism to Language-Based Discrimination

When we enter our classrooms, we must be vigilant about understanding how linguicism shapes the language that we teach, how we teach it, and how language learning is evaluated. Often, linguicism is so embedded in the logic of schooling that it is challenging to recognize and to address (Milner, 2017). In schools and in classrooms, research has widely documented that students of color, Indigenous students, and refugee and migrant students face discrimination on the basis of which languages they use and how they use these languages. The language skills of these students are evaluated against a normative standard that corresponds with the ways of using language common in White, middle-class, mainstream, U.S. communities (Paris & Alim, 2014). It is rare that this standard is questioned, in part, because of the historical legacy of how language has been used as a tool for discrimination historically in schools.

In the nineteenth century United States, laws prohibiting teaching reading and writing to the enslaved were commonplace as a way to stem abolition efforts as well as insurrection and slave revolts. Similarly, the erasure of Indigenous language and culture through the widespread use of English-only models to educate Native American children remained a frequent practice from the seventeenth century (Baker-Bell, 2020a; de los Ríos et al., 2019). Indeed, American Indian boarding schools in the United States and Canada, in which English was the singular mode of instruction, prefigured the English-only instructional efforts commonplace in U.S. schools today. The history of these schools, now widely recognized as settings in which violence was perpetrated on Indigenous children, cannot be separated from today's instructional efforts to educate multilingual children and children of color (Patel, 2019). Both have been motivated by the misguided belief that other language resources should be replaced with mainstream English ones. Of course, it is worth noting that while models of instruction that reify monolingualism are dominant, education efforts in the United States historically have not always focused on monolingualism. Bilingualism has always been present and runs as a parallel strand through our education systems. Early conversion efforts by U.S. missionaries often took place in languages other than English, and many U.S. schools were bilingual through the advent of World War I (Crawford, 2000). Yet, what is important to note is that bilingualism in these instances was often in the service of other forms of dominance.

These historical examples—even those that have favored bilingualism—represent forms of settler colonialism, which still in the present, commonly motivates language policy in U.S. schools (Patel, 2019). These historical practices and their present-day legacies dehumanize and harm learners who are unable to bring their whole linguistic selves to the classroom. They also create schools that ignore or actively suppress linguistic richness, which is harmful to all learners. In the United States, Canada, South Africa, and in other settings where Indigenous language has faced erasure, much needs to be done to retroactively address these harms and to stop perpetuating reductive language teaching in today's schools.

Linguicism remains a powerful force in today's classrooms. Take, for example, the U.S. Common Core College and Career Ready Standards for language for upper grade students (6th–12th grade), which emphasize the teaching of "standard English" by suggesting that students should have a "command of the conventions of standard English grammar and usage when writing or speaking" (National Governors Association Center for Best Practices & Council of Chief State School Officers, 2010, p. 51). In focusing on this narrow goal, Common Core standards position the language of White, middle-class students as the ideal for all, which has the effect of diminishing the language resources and practices of others, such as emergent multilingual learners or users of Black English language (Baker-Bell, 2020a; Gutiérrez et al., 2009; Valdés, 2004). Instructional standards, whether at the state or district level, have been interpreted and used to inform instruction, which has resulted in an over-emphasis on correcting language practices viewed as deviating from standardized English—a subtractive approach (Valenzuela, 2005). Subtractive approaches often have the goal of assimilation and thus can be especially damaging for multilingual students and for members of minoritized speech communities. This is in contrast to attempts to meet the Standards that take an additive approach.

Additive approaches aim to develop students' linguistic resources by adding language as students master new content while also inviting students' existing language resources into the classroom. Of course, additive approaches do not always play out this way, and we should be wary of instructional efforts that only seek to add majoritized language to students' existing repertoires and stop short of bringing in and nurturing the development of students' preexisting and other language resources in the classroom. Framings of student achievement that emphasize "achievement gaps" between minoritized and non-minoritized students on the basis of scores on standardized assessments of reading are also evidence of the widespread linguicism still present in education (Kendi, 2019). Others, such as Milner (2017) focused instead on "opportunity gaps" to emphasize differences in the educational opportunities historically afforded to students of color (see also Ladson-Billings, 2006). In the realm of language teaching, for example, students of color and other language-minoritized youth are routinely denied the opportunity to participate in settings in which language is taught as an authentic and meaningful social practice; student activities like debate league or model U.N. as well as advanced placement or honors classes routinely exclude or are unwelcoming to learners of color.

Arguments about language use in classrooms often focus on language form. It helps here to make a distinction between using standardized English to discuss high-level concepts and using standardized English to make simple requests, such as asking to leave the classroom or to open a window. To say that a student used standardized English does not describe the nature or purpose of an interaction, just the format (i.e., English and specific grammatical rules) in which it was delivered, and the perceived prestige associated with using something that is the "standard." Other Englishes and certainly other languages could easily be used to complete these same requests. Yet in classrooms, we often teach a standardized form of English aligned with state instructional standards, signaling that we value this language over others. Standardized English is not a neutral ideal, but is instead a term associated with Whiteness and class distinctions. Its preferred use in classrooms validates the identities of some and denigrates that of others. By contrast, we propose that educators offer new expressive resources to students, rather than attempt to replace the language that students bring with more standardized varieties. For example, when we teach the language of the disciplines or of text, using language-awareness inquiry routines that draw attention to language features and choices, we can support all students' learning and bolster student self-expression. These instructional goals aim to facilitate all students working together to construct meaning.

CONCEPTIONS THAT PROMOTE EQUITABLE LANGUAGE INSTRUCTION: APPROACHES THAT RESIST LANGUAGE HIERARCHIES

What Does This Mean for Instruction?

Linguicism will continue into the instruction of the future if we do not begin to address it today. We turn in the subsequent sections to instructional practices that address historical and present manifestations of linguicism in language instruction as a means of demonstrating how we might teach for a more equitable future.

Questioning Our Own Taken-For-Granted Assumptions About Language. When we enter classrooms as educators, we each bring assumptions about language shaped by our own experiences as learners, by the cultural and racial communities in which we have used language, and the professional preparation we have received (Milner, 2007a). Each of us is navigating personal beliefs about language as well as the generally hidden practices and policies that are embedded in schools and directly influence how we teach and evaluate the learning of language (Gist, 2017; McClain et al., 2021). Given these implicit factors, we have found that the reflective work of examining beliefs about language is complex and often best done in community with others. This may involve teacher professional learning communities where we examine together what language we plan to teach and question why we plan to teach that language, with our focus being on teaching language that enables students' participation and empowerment.

Teaching Language as a Tool for Critiquing and Dismantling Linguicism and Other Oppressive Systems. An under-examined aspect of the language used in school and across disciplines is its potential to describe complex phenomena, such as social inequality, that are often not visible to us in the absence of language to talk about them. For example, we may have experienced discrimination on the basis of our own language use—perhaps because we have been perceived to have an accent or to be a speaker of a minoritized English such as Southern American English—but lacked the language to describe this systematic discrimination to others. Having the term *linguicism* offers a way to discuss with others how these episodes of discrimination are not isolated, but rather part of a systemic way in which discrimination operates. For our students, using language-awareness inquiry routines to make social inequality visible is a powerful practice that enables equity (McClain et al., 2021). As literacy scholar Gholdy Muhammad (2020) underscored, the purpose of this teaching should be twofold: "to make sense of injustice but also to work toward social transformation" (p. 120).

Ms. Foster-Yu viewed one of her roles as supporting her students to make meaning of complex societal issues, and to support them in being changemakers. Beyond lesson planning that aims to simply teach language, she was focused on teaching language that would support students to trouble injustice. In the next example, Ms. Foster-Yu engages her students in a language-awareness inquiry routine in which they must attend to the role of language in communicating possible actions and in grappling with injustice. Ms. Foster-Yu had not initially planned to discuss the George Floyd case with her young students. However, after overhearing students discussing Floyd on the playground and communicating with parents and guardians, she became aware that the majority of her students had been in conversations about these events in home, church, and community settings. This lesson is one of many in which the class worked to process their thinking. As a responsive educator, Ms. Foster-Yu sought to support her students by teaching language as a tool for making sense of the world. Consider how she scaffolds learning by providing language for the task of critiquing inequality in transformational ways:

Ms. Foster-Yu: So, yesterday was a very hard day in the United States. I know many of you have been talking with moms, dads, and grandmas about this. So, Derek Chauvin was convicted of murdering George Floyd. But, the part that I need your help with is that we still have a problem because Black and Brown people are still more likely to be killed in the United States than others. This is still something that in the United States—as a country and as a community—we have a problem with. As a community of little friends who will grow up and become adults, we will have to change this together. We can do this together because our community doesn't have to be this way. We can make it better. How many of you want to make it better? How many of you want to make a change? [kids raised hands] *What does it mean to "make change" in the way I'm using it now? It's not like getting coins back from a cashier, so. . . .*

Gracie: Well, I think it's like to do something different, so make it better.

Ms. Foster-Yu: Great, so "make change" is actually kind of a funny phrase—it can mean different things: breaking a larger amount of money into a smaller amount, say getting four quarters for a dollar, is making change. But, just now, Gracie told us it can also mean making something better. This is called *polysemy*—when a word or phrase can mean a few different things.

Monica: I do—but I also want adults to.

Ms. Foster-Yu: Okay, Monica, let's start with us: What are some things we can do in our lives to make it better? If you want to share, you can say: "*We can make change by________. (writes phrase on small white board) You can add anything you want. Remember, even kids can do things to make change!"*

Luis: Write letters, like when we wrote to Dr. Walker (the principal). Maybe, we can write to the police and ask for help?

Ms. Foster-Yu: Great, Luis, your mom is a police officer, so maybe she can help us think of what to say? (Luis nodding) What else? Anybody?

Yuwen: I think we can make change by being friends to everyone, and when we're adults we can be different. We can make things more equal.

Ms. Foster-Yu: I like how you said that, Yuwen. We do need to think about how we interact with others. I like the idea of imagining ourselves as the adults we'd like to be, because I know you can make change! We know it won't be easy, but in this class our friends do hard things. You said we can make things more "equal." *Have you heard the word, "equality"?*

Geraldo: I have! It's like "igualdad," which means fair.

Ms. Foster-Yu: Fab, Geraldo, you heard equality and knew it sounded like a word you knew in Spanish! I like those connections! You knew it meant fair.

Geraldo: So, igualdad is like if we make sure that all kids get to have breakfast and lunch.

Ms. Foster-Yu: Great, so equality is when all children have access to the same nutrition, so all children should have access to food. We can make change by giving people equal access to food.

Bowen: We can make change by thinking of others before we do things. For example, I can think about how it would feel to be you if I call you a name or something, maybe I could say that I was sorry and then try to make it better?

Ms. Foster-Yu: Right, remember we called this "perspective taking"? You used the phrase "for example." Why did Bowen do that, do you think?

Monica: He was telling us about a time we can think of others.

Ms. Foster-Yu: Exactly—when you say, "for example" the people listening know you're telling them something that is more specific, giving me an example of what you mean. This is something you can do in your writing, too.

Clearly, the focus of this lesson is not primarily to teach language. Instead, Ms. Foster-Yu explores a complex topic that is meaningful to students and, along the way, teaches language to support all students' participation in this activity and develop their curiosity about how language can synthesize or capture ideas and empower her students. This calls for the use of diverse verb tenses (e.g., you heard, you can) and opens the door for joint engagement in speculative talk. To support her students, she unpacks a polysemous phrase that she knows may challenge her students designated as multilingual learners and offers a sentence frame to scaffold students' use of syntax production that communicates meaning clearly ("*We can make change by________.*"). She highlights the use of a connective phrase "for example" and links this to its communicative function, offering students a phrase that is useful in speech and in writing. She also incorporates new terms—equality—and offers students the opportunity to connect this to first-language knowledge.

Ms. Foster-Yu teaches and scaffolds students' language production as a component of authentic content study—what Muhammad (2020) referred to as using language as a "conduit to liberation" (p. 89). We have found in our school-based work that focusing on conceptually rich and engaging content leads to more opportunities for language teaching. In fact, without engaging content matched to students' developmental levels, it is challenging to teach language at all, simply because the curriculum affords too few opportunities for rich language use. School content generates a fertile space for revealing the role language choice plays in sensemaking. Language-awareness inquiry routines promote language teaching because they reveal how language is being used to capture specific ideas and ways of sensemaking in a particular field or area of study, and in so doing parse how language is used for specific aims.

Ms. Foster Yu's language-awareness inquiry routine also unpacks the relationships between language and power, another central component of critiquing linguicism in the classroom. Alim (2010) referred to the skills we develop in students to examine the relations between language and power as *critical language awareness*. Uccelli and Phillips Galloway (2017) extended this concept to refer to the skills we develop in students to critically evaluate the ways in which they and others use language to assert authority and establish power differentials as *critical rhetorical flexibility*. The addition of the word "flexibility" underscores that the goal of language teaching in classrooms is not to promote the robotic use of mainstream language resources but rather to develop students' awareness of the multiple language resources available to them as part of increasing their linguistic flexibility. To be flexible, students must understand and be aware of various language functions, which can be revealed through language-awareness inquiry routines.

To make this concrete, let's turn to another example. An 8th-grade science teacher, Mr. Sosa worked with his students to communicate how a solution of water and sugar could become saturated, or so laden with sugar that it would no longer dissolve. He hoped that his students would not only be able to explain this concept using the language of the text and of the discipline, but also would be able to communicate this concept to the 5th-grade science buddies that each student had been assigned. The application tasks for the unit were twofold: (1) students would produce a written explanation of how a solution became saturated as a result of the titration process by labeling a diagram and using the language of chemistry to annotate, and (2) students would produce a short picture book to explain all the scientific terms they were learning to younger students. This picture book would contain some disciplinary terms from chemistry, but Mr. Sosa wanted his students to be able to use their range of communicative resources to describe the concepts. As a result, he encouraged students to use examples from everyday life and language learned in a range of settings and languages other than English to communicate with their buddies. Far from a narrow focus on content-area language and standardized English to the exclusion of other language resources, Mr. Sosa's assignments centered the language resources of his students in ways that sought to use these as integral to science learning. The result was that they became more flexible users of language, able to explain core concepts to a diverse audience.

Mr. Sosa hadn't always taught this way, however. In fact, in his early days of teaching he internalized a view of language that reified linguistic hierarchies. These views had come from his own experiences as a Cuban-American immigrant. He was told by his teachers that he should never use his Spanish in the classroom, and that the English he was using—which he was acquiring through interactions in his neighborhood—was not welcome at school. He recalled his early days of teaching when he was quick to correct students' language even when the communicative skills that students displayed were impressive. Over time, he came to realize that this instruction only served to silence some students in his classroom and did not really reflect how science was done; after all, he had worked in many chemistry labs where scientific language intermingled with language learned in other settings. Aligned with his experience in linguistically permeable professional environments, his teaching now encourages and integrates a range of communicative resources in the service of learning.

Centering Minoritized Linguistic Resources as Counter-Stories to Linguicism. Too often, the language that students bring to the classroom is not reflected in the texts read, the writing completed, or teachers' expectations of what discussion should sound like in the classroom. In part, this is a result of the canonical texts used in classrooms and curriculums. These texts often contain few authentic representations of language-in-use. Another contributor to the marginalization of some students' language resources, however, is the parameters we establish for writing and speaking in ways that favor White Mainstream English. Solórzano and Yosso (2001) as well as Kinloch and colleagues (2020) have suggested that this can be addressed by inviting counternarratives that make visible the power and utility of language resources typically excluded in schools into the classroom. For example, counternarratives may come in the form of bilingual texts or those that make use of non-mainstream English. Texts that are print, digital, and oral offer a greater opportunity for incorporating sources relevant to a specific content focus. Such texts for young children include *Honey Baby Sugar Child* (Duncan, 2005) and *Honey, I Love* (Greenfield, 2016), both of which center the richness of Black English language.

The first pages of *Honey, I Love* read:

> "My cousin comes to visit
> and you know he's from the South
> 'cause every word he says
> just kind of slides out of his mouth.
>
> I like the way
> he whistles
> and I like the way
> he walks
>
> But honey, let me tell you that
> I LOVE the way he talks
> I love the way my cousin talks"

As you read the language, two things are evident: The protagonist is celebrating language of minoritized speakers in the U.S. South and speaking to readers using Black English language—a powerful discourse of personhood and place often absent in elementary grade curriculum.

Creating opportunities for students to use language learned in other settings when speaking and writing, and thereby encouraging students to use all their linguistic resources, makes counternarratives visible. For example, studies have demonstrated that when students are invited to use a wider array of language resources, youth used Black English language to enhance learning by making sense in the content areas (Lee, 2006) and expressing their perspective (Wynter-Hoyte & Smith, 2020). Indeed, Mr. Sosa noted that as part of creating counternarratives in the classroom, he allowed his students to use both Black and Puerto Rican Englishes, and his students were better able to explain concepts and took ownership over their learning, often seeking to plug gaps in their peers' understanding.

This research offers a counterpoint to dominant views of Black English language, which often result in providing Black students with "remediation" in the form of skills-focused interventions and denying them access to opportunities to engage in conceptually rich curriculum. This inclusion of counternarratives is not only a matter of representation, but also is essential to affirming the identities and belonging of students in the classroom (Love, 2019; Souto-Manning, 2021). In Ms. Foster-Yu's class, she called upon students to share their own experiences with racism and linguicism and centered these stories in her lessons. She would frequently return to students' own examples, saying things like "I'm thinking about what Geraldo told us about how he felt when he was told he couldn't use Spanish in school—that was really sad for him. Do you think this character might be feeling this way? Could inviting students to use their language learned at home be helpful, do you think? This is called being 'inclusive.'" These conversations both validated students' heritage language resources and taught students language to help them talk about the ideas they were grappling with.

Eliminating Language Proficiency as a Barrier to Participation in the Classroom's Learning Community. In many school settings, language proficiency operates as a mechanism for denying access to curricular opportunities, like chances to read rich texts that are aligned to students' developmental levels (not just to a reading level), to participate in complex discussions, or to be given leadership opportunities. An important first step to eliminating these barriers is examining how students are grouped in your classroom and how those groupings impact learning opportunity (McClain et al., 2021).

Often, reading levels or scores from English language proficiency tests are used not just to inform instruction, but also to place students into groupings. These groupings can be useful occasionally to provide targeted instruction, although we still lack clear evidence to drive a precise understanding of what types of groupings are most impactful for what activities. We have observed that grouping students heterogeneously for the vast majority of the instructional day allows for more student exposure to peers as language models and democratizes access to the curriculum. In Ms. Foster-Yu's class, students were initially grouped by reading levels derived from an initial benchmarking assessment. Over time, however, she began to see how this practice limited her students' opportunities to learn from one another. Students who were as beginning readers and often still in the process of learning English were grouped together, with few opportunities to interact with peers who could access more complex texts. This meant that discussions were less rich for all students in the classroom. Her greater worry, however, was that some students were developing identities as readers and thinkers, while students in groups comprised of beginning readers seemed to regard themselves as "non-readers." She wondered what this meant for her students' continued education and was concerned that she was creating mechanisms that could exclude some children from the academic community. Seeking to change this model, she committed to using heterogenous groupings whenever possible. Slowly, this move began to have an impact. She began to notice that there were more discussions among all students in the classroom and the assumption that only a few students could answer her comprehension questions quickly faded. Reflecting on and using a range of groupings is critical for avoiding language barriers to learning, and ensuring all students can participate, meaningfully exchange ideas, and develop rich representations of content being covered in classrooms.

Planning for Action for Educators

Tips for Instruction That Supports Language as Resource for Learning and Resists Language Hierarchies

- ***Use instructional materials that depict positively the linguistic resources of all students in a classroom; these can be print, audio, or visual texts.***
  - Using bilingual texts or those that make use of non-mainstream English such as *Honey, I Love.*
- ***Emphasize how all language is useful and important for communication.***
  - Modeling listening to understand by consistently allowing students to finish speaking and encouraging all students to do the same. (Ms. Foster Yu: "I want to see you listening to Kiera to understand what she is saying. . . . Please let Kiera complete her thought, Nora.")
  - Modeling and encouraging practices for confirming comprehension. (Ms. Foster Yu: "I think I heard you say . . ."; "Let's summarize what we've heard so far. . . . What did I miss?")
  - Recognizing and validating linguistic knowledge from other Englishes, such as Black English language, and other languages. (Darius: "Juan's pretending like he grown and tellin' me what to do!" Ms. Foster-Yu: "I bet that's frustrating, let's remember we're each responsible for ourselves, Juan"; Ms. Foster-Yu: "What do you remember from the story?" Darius: "They be buildin' the houses all day. . . ." Ms. Foster-Yu: "Right, what else do you remember?")

- ***Offer students the opportunity to use all linguistic resources when completing learning activities. Even in states with so-called "English-only" mandates where teachers are not able to teach in a language other than English, students are not barred from using all linguistic resources, including those learned in an additional language, in the classroom.***
  - » Creating assignments like Mr. Sosa's short picture book assignment made by 8th-graders for younger students to explain scientific terms using language from other spaces
- ***Prioritize teaching students to be critical and flexible users of language over simply teaching the language of school or the disciplines. Imagine preparing students to be full and active participants in social and professional aspects of society, rather than just preparing them for workforce and secondary school participation.***
  - » Offering new linguistic options and inviting students' existing linguistic knowledge. (Ms. Foster Yu: "What are some other ways to say 'sad' in English or in other languages?"; "I want to teach you a new way to say 'mad'; you can say 'enraged' if you're really, really mad!"; "Oh, neat, Juan, just gave us the word for that in Spanish"; "How can I say that in Spanish?")
  - » Reformulating language rather than correcting speech. (Mara: "I eated the whole thing!" Ms. Foster-Yu: "What? That muffin was huge, I can't believe you ate the whole thing!")
  - » Teaching specific terms to talk about linguistic prejudice and other forms of discrimination and exclusion (e.g., linguicism, unconscious bias)
  - » Using language awareness inquiry routines to draw attention to specific language features (words, ways ideas are linked, and organizational frames and structures of language use) and ways language is used to assert authority and establish power differentials
- ***Use both linguistically heterogenous and homogenous groupings, moving between groupings of students who are users of the same and different languages, that increase rich content conversations and a focus on the meaningful exchange of ideas.***

Model these practices to create a classroom where all students are learning how to welcome the language resources of others, feel comfortable sharing their own language resources, focus on the meaningful exchange of ideas, and unpack language as a resource for learning and how it instantiates power.

CLOSING THOUGHTS ON VALUING DIVERSE LANGUAGE RESOURCES FOR LEARNING

In this chapter, we reflect on the multiple purposes for language instruction. In linguistically fluid classrooms, students are not only engaged in learning language as part of content mastery, but also as a medium for critiquing and transforming inequities. We view this as critical work for today's teachers, but equally important, essential to addressing historical, insidious, and persistent language ideologies that reify hierarchical views of language and serve to limit the language we teach in schools in ways that are harmful for students. Unfortunately, these views often persist into the present. For all of us, this is about creating futures where students are able to marshal language in order to express thinking, make new meanings, and contest injustice.

CHAPTER 2 CLOSING REFLECTION

Consider your reflections at the start of this chapter and ask: In what ways do I/can I help students to examine power–language relations in my instruction? Think about a lesson you have taught in the past that might have linguicism embedded in it. What language-awareness inquiry questions might you ask now to get students to be more reflective of power–language relations? How do I contribute to unequal power–language relations in my own teaching?

CHAPTER 3

Language as a Dichotomy Versus Language as a Continuum

> **CONCEPTIONS THAT PROMOTE EQUITABLE LANGUAGE TEACHING**
>
> Language exists on a continuum with no clear boundaries between the language of school and other settings. For this reason, instruction in classrooms must allow all students to draw on their entire linguistic repertoires.

Two of the four teachers that comprise the 7th-grade team at Alder Glen Middle School sit in the teachers' room engaged in deep discussion: Mr. Washington—a science teacher—explains that an important aspect of the instruction he provides in his classroom is teaching the formal language of school, which he believes is categorically distinct from the language that is used in outside-of-school settings. Mr. Washington describes to his colleagues in the teachers' room that language can be clearly sorted into that which is connected to school tasks and that which is conversational. Talking to Ms. Morris, the social studies teacher, he says, "My classroom is a central context for students to practice the language of school, and I frequently correct students' use of language used in outside-of-school settings." Mr. Washington argues that this is a matter of equity: Mr. Washington explains that as a Latino man, he knows what it feels like to face discrimination and he views teaching formal language, which he interchangeably calls "Standard English," "appropriate language," and "academic language" as equipping his students with linguistic tools to navigate majority-White educational and professional settings.

Ms. Morris feels differently. She responds that there is no such thing as language that is just "academic" or "formal." To Ms. Morris, the "language of school" refers to the language features that have a higher probability of occurring in school texts than in other contexts of language use, although this language might also be used orally and in outside-of-school settings. From her perspective, classroom-based learning requires students to use all language resources to make meaning from texts and to negotiate new understandings of content. To her, allowing students to use their broader linguistic repertoires is a hallmark of equitable language teaching. Indeed, her own linguistic experiences as a Latina Afro-Brazilian multilingual learner speaking Portuguese and English have underscored for her the importance of allowing students to access all the language available to them as they learn. While the tone is respectful, when Ms. Ruiz—the 7th-grade English teacher—enters the teachers' room, it is evident that her colleagues are struggling to reach a consensus. Ms. Ruiz, a Spanish- and English-speaking Latina, begins to think to herself about her own understanding of equity in language teaching and whether her pedagogical approach is more aligned with Mr. Washington's or Ms. Morris's.

CHAPTER 3 REFLECTION

Take a moment before we move on to consider your own views on language use and teaching in your classroom. In what ways do your views align with Mr. Washington's? In what ways do your views align with Ms. Morris's?

Mr. Washington and Ms. Morris, while both motivated by the goal of creating equitable learning opportunities for students, hold two distinct views of language teaching that are challenging to reconcile. While Mr. Washington advocates for a binary view of language, Ms. Morris views language use as more fluid. In our own work in school settings, we routinely encounter these divergent perspectives. In this chapter, we tackle the commonly evoked dichotomy that positions the language of school as categorically distinct from language used for communication in outside-of-school settings, which often has the effect of positioning students' own linguistic resources as unwelcome in the classroom, particularly disadvantaging students who are speakers of Black English language as well as multilingual youth. We argue, however, that there is no language that is solely used in classrooms, and all of students' linguistic resources are useful for the task of learning at school. We discuss, in particular, the concept of *languaging* or using language as a tool for participation in social actions in classrooms (Swain, 2006). Because the goal of instruction is to enable students to participate fully in language interactions, we must begin by reimagining what makes a skilled language user.

WHAT MAKES A SKILLED LANGUAGE USER?: A CONTINUUM PERSPECTIVE

Think for just a moment about the most skilled user of language that you know. It is very likely that the person who came to mind first was not someone who only brings skills in using academic language. For most of us, a skilled language user is someone who can draw across a continuum of language resources flexibly and fluidly to make a point and to get across a message. Take this short segment of text from an article appearing in *The Atlantic* by lauded writer Ta-Nehisi Coates (2017):

> Kaepernick did not inaugurate his protest in hopes of helping elect more centrist Democrats, or any kind of Democrat. That said, he was not immune to compromise. When his initial efforts were met with disdain and deemed disrespectful, *he actually consulted a group of veterans to see how he might better pursue a protest. That is the origin of Kaepernick kneeling,* and the fact that it too has been met with scoffs points to a deeper problem. If young people attempting to board a bus are unacceptable, if gathering on the National Mall is verboten, if preaching nonviolence gets you harassed by your own government and then killed, if a protest founded in consultation with military veterans is offensive, then what specific manner of protest is White America willing to endure?
>
> It's almost as if the manner of protest isn't the real problem.

Coates is a skilled language user who deftly combines vocabulary, sentence structures, and text organization common in academic print with those used in oral language. For example, the italicized phrase "That is the origin of Kaepernick kneeling" refers back to the previous portion of the text "he actually consulted a group of veterans to see how he might better pursue a protest." This use of a complex chain of reference is a common strategy in academic writing to avoid having to rewrite a referent multiple times in a text. Of course, this is also a strategy used in spoken language, as is the use of a conjunction ("it's," "isn't") for rhetorical impact in the last sentence. We can imagine Coates speaking these words, or we can read them in his essay; yet, the use of phrases familiar from oral language ("that said," "it's almost as if") supports our comprehension regardless of the medium and makes us feel engaged with Coates's message. The organization of the text segment reflects a format common in school essays: The body text offers an elaboration of Coates' argument and the final sentence offers a summary of Coates's conclusions. The use of an offset single sentence at the conclusion for rhetorical impact is not common in school texts. However, this format is a well-known strategy from argumentative oral discourse and from preaching. Coates draws across multiple genres of written and spoken discourse to increase his rhetorical impact. In this example, he is *languaging*, or using language to complete a social action (Swain, 2006).

Languaging: What Does It Look and Sound Like?

If we draw on the models provided by skilled writers like Coates, then our goal for students is not that they learn to draw only on language resources like those traditionally found in print, but rather that they can move across the continuum of language resources with fluidity and flexibility—both skills that are developed over time through opportunities to use language in more dynamic ways. We refer to the practice of using language—academic or otherwise—as *languaging* (Swain, 2006). Like Coates, our goal is always to communicate our thinking and understanding to others. This type of language use is not captured by references to academic language, school language, or content area language, all of which are more static conceptions of language. We view the use of language in classrooms as social action that achieves both the communication of our understandings of content and concepts *as well as* our various identities.

Language-awareness inquiry routines allow educators to unpack languaging practices frequently used in classrooms, often by aiding students to think metalinguistically about language (i.e., reflect on and analyze language choices and use) and to explore the use of language for transformational purposes. To develop this idea of languaging, we consider two languaging practices common in schools: understanding multiple perspectives, including those of peers, and making thinking visible through language choices. Each serves as a moment to engage in language-awareness routines that help our students to see that language use in classrooms involves drawing on a continuum of language resources. This is both a metalinguistic activity, as students are engaging in actively puzzling through how language is used and why, and a transformational activity, because students are asked to consider power dynamics embedded in how language is used.

To see languaging at work, we turn to Ms. Morris's 7th-grade social studies classroom, where her students are working in small groups to draw links between civil rights movements of the 1960s and those occurring today. In this first example, students share perspectives in preparation for a debate.

Louis: Listen up, right, so I'm not sayin' that I think it's totally the same. I mean like back in the day, it was more obvious. Racism was more obvious because people were getting killed and stuff, but, like, now it's more structural, so probably people can't see it and that's why people don't think that, like, the BLM [Black Lives Matter] is a civil rights thing.

Ms. Morris: That's one perspective. I'm sure there are a few others in this group. Does anyone have a perspective, an opinion, that is different from the one that we heard from Louis?

Marcia: I don't think that's right. My thinking is that people see it as a civil rights issue, but that not everyone, or some people anyways, don't want to do anything about it. They wanna' jus' just keep it like they be doin' it now.

Louis: So, you think that people get that we still have racism? I mean 'cause . . .

Janelle: Right, so what about being color-blind? Isn't that people not seeing racism? I think that's people not seeing racism, in my opinion. My perspective is that racism isn't obvious to everybody like [it is] to people of color.

Marcia: Ya, I think it's not that people don't be seein' racism, it's that they don' wanna do anything different. However, Louis appears to think people don't wanna be seeing it, that's what he said.

In this example, students move back and forth between the language commonly found in print and that found more often in oral language as part of a social interaction in which they are negotiating conceptual understandings. For example, students make use of abstract vocabulary, including nominalized words—racism, structural, and opinion. They also invoke common markers of perspective and uncertainty common in text ("in my opinion," "my perspective is . . ." "However, Louis appears to think . . ."). Yet, students also bring in language used in oral speech ("They wanna jus' just keep it like they be doin' it now"). Ms. Morris supports students' sensemaking by underscoring the activity at hand: perspective taking. She used the language-awareness inquiry prompt: *"Does anyone have a perspective, an opinion, that is different from the one that we heard from Louis?"* We note that "perspective" and "opinion" are synonyms used to describe common activities in argumentation. Ms. Morris brings in both to highlight for students the language at their disposal and offer them a definition to support their grasp of the content. Ms. Morris simultaneously positions students to articulate alternative perspectives, opening the door for Marcia to enter the conversation.

This fluid movement between language traditionally found in print and oral exchanges is also evident in a second example as Louis and Armando work with classmate, Lorena, to help her to articulate her perspective and actively participate in the classroom community.

Louis: I still don't get what you mean, really.

Armando: Are you sayin' that, maybe, it's not so clear because some people think that racism isn't something that they're doing?

Lorena: No, I guess, I mean that racism's not something that you KNOW you are doing all the time, you're just reacting. So, ya, I think that's maybe what you said, 'Mando?

Ms. Morris: So, what I hear you saying, Lorena and Armando, seems to have a good deal of overlap. Do you hear that also?

Armando: [To Lorena] Okay, so you are saying that racism can be like an, what we called, unconscious bias. You are acting in ways that are racist, but you're not, like, conscious of it?

Ms. Morris: Is that what you were thinking of, Lorena? *That phrase we say in the text, "unconscious bias," do you remember what it meant?*

Lorena: Right. People have unconscious bias and so act racist without recognizing that they are doing something that has consequences for somebody else.

> *Ms. Morris:* Nice, I like how you phrased that "people have x, and so . . ." that's a great structure for explaining how ideas are related to others. You clearly linked unconscious bias to what it means for peoples' actions. Can you offer some other examples of how that plays out exactly? Not just Lorena, anybody can tell us. Just get us started and we can all work together to get our ideas out. And, the examples don't have to be from school.

In this example, students support a classmate to articulate her perspective as part of the social interactions taking place in the classroom. The conversation relies on a continuum of language resources that are commonly taken up inside and outside of academic conversations in school, but, through specific language choices, sets Lorena up to fully make visible her understanding of the issues at hand. Both Armando and Ms. Morris work with Lorena to match newly learned conceptual language (unconscious bias) to her purpose and make frequent attempts to reiterate her perspective as a method for creating alignment across the group (e.g., "Okay, so you are saying [to Lorena] that racism can be like an, what we called, unconscious bias. . . . Is that what you were thinking of, Lorena?"). In both examples from Ms. Morris's classroom, the result of this more fluid approach is greater access to sensemaking activities for all students and inclusion of all students' linguistic resources. This approach invites students into both the classroom's linguistic community and to the intellectual work taking place, setting the stage for creating classrooms where all language—of all students—is viewed as a functional resource for learning.

Ms. Morris also makes this activity less about individual language use, underscoring the way in which languaging is a social activity in which the diverse language resources of students working together can all be used for sensemaking. Ms. Morris prepared for this lesson by selecting metalinguistic language that enabled her and her students to refer to aspects of reasoning and argumentation ("opinion," "perspective"). However, these language features also reflected her larger aims for the lesson (i.e., transformational aims). To that end, Ms. Morris selected language that would support students in questioning existing power structures as well as labeling systemic factors that maintain them (like "unconscious bias"). Not every lesson will overtly focus on concepts that address issues of power, such as prejudice and unconscious bias. However, language choices themselves are always situated within power relations, with language features intended to disseminate information in ways that are specific to a particular community of language users and thus invite in or exclude. Transformational aims that make visible the role of language in crafting exclusive and inclusive spaces is central to pedagogy that supports linguistic fluidity and critical and conscious languaging.

THE PROBLEM WITH BINARIES IN LANGUAGE TEACHING AND USE

To illustrate how language is used flexibly as a communicative resource, imagine, for example, stepping into Ms. Morris's classroom. As students discuss social studies concepts, you would see them engaged in the use of language learned in home and community settings and the language they are learning from exploring academic print. Some students might be using Spanish to engage in *translanguaging* (García & Wei, 2014)—moving between two languages fluidly in ways that align with a view of multilingual language resources as integrated—as part of making sense of new concepts and content. The dialogue might look and sound something like this as a group of students—many multilingual—work to collaboratively compose an answer to a question posed by Ms. Morris about the impact of Jim Crow laws in the U.S. South:

Armando: Right, ya, so y'all said that the civil rights of the people, they be stepped on by the Jim Crows. I'm gonna write: "Black Americans faced significant challenges because of Jim Crow Laws."

Lorena: Si, bueno, we also add something about the vote rights, an ejemplo.

Armando: Ya, okay. So, let's put that here [pointing at third sentence in the paragraph that the group has been co-constructing]. Hey, back off, brah [to Michael who is leaning over him to reach the keyboard].

Michael: I want to add that like you're needing to add that the big point is that these laws were like just for them, like directed at Black people, like to make things harder to prevent them getting stuff. Write [to Armando] "Jim Crow laws that prevented voter participation were a reaction to the worry from White people that Black people would gain more access to economic things, like education and jobs."

Janie: I'd say "concern" not "worry". . . . Change the word.

Michael: I'd say now that we have, like, the Juan Crow laws. . . . They're doin' the same damn sh . . . stuff.

Armando: So, what do I add?

Janie: I'd say that "As much as things change they stay the same: Today, in the South, we have laws that discriminate against other people, like Latinos. These laws and policies need to change to make society more fair."

Students could have written responses that contained a combination of more academic and more everyday language. At times, this was the case in Ms. Morris's classroom. In this instance, however, Janie steered her peers to produce a text that mirrored that of the academic sources read in the classroom. This reflects both her interpretation of the audience and the task. In other instances, Janie and her peers interpreted the audience differently and elected to use language they commonly relied on in outside-of-school speech communities. By creating assignments in which students were tasked with speaking with different audiences, Ms. Morris invited responses that engaged different language resources and used these language resources flexibly, allowing students to determine which language to use to achieve their communicative goals.

How did Ms. Morris come to adopt this flexible stance that allowed her students to use all of their language resources? First, in her teaching she questions a series of binaries that perpetuate rigid separations between language resources. These binaries can create a kind of paralysis in some teachers, like Mr. Washington, who wants to teach for linguistic equity but who also fears that without an emphasis on mainstream English and his constant corrections, his students will not be able to fulfill their academic potential and professional success due to societal prejudices. The two binaries we discuss next show how language-awareness inquiry routines might craft a space where students are empowered and where the language of school tasks is not used as a tool to marginalize other language resources, but as a springboard for language dissection and critique. In the field of education and in the United States more broadly, we love binaries. In part, this is because they serve to organize our thinking. The reality, though, is that reducing language to binaries of classroom language and outside-of-school language is an unhelpful practice that obscures the lived reality of language use, which is much more dynamic.

Binary 1. A common challenge we encounter is the way academic language is equated with "appropriate" language for school (Alim et al., 2016; Paris, 2012). Indeed, educators we've worked with, including Mr. Washington, spoke about their understanding of so-called "academic language" as the only "appropriate" language for classroom settings (Neugebauer & Heineke, 2020). The problem with this way of thinking is that all other language, including students' home language resources, is cast as "inappropriate." Critics of academic language instruction rightfully underscore how, when academic language is used simply as a proxy for standardized English or White Mainstream English and presented as the sole language appropriate in schools, this instruction only serves to further marginalize the language of some groups of students and further entrench linguicism in education (Baker-Bell, 2017, 2020a). This exclusion ultimately threatens students' sense of classroom belonging (Souto-Manning, 2021). We can easily imagine how this might have played out in Ms. Morris's classroom. She could have rigidly enforced a norm in which students were asked to use only the language of schooling, placing a heavy emphasis on the language learned from the texts used in her unit. Instead, what we see is an emphasis on fluidly and flexibly, space for the use of all language resources, regardless of whether this language was learned in school or elsewhere.

Viewing school language simply as a language of "appropriateness" also denies that it serves a range of communicative functions and reinforces an understanding of language use as rigid and context-bound. The message that students receive is that the language taught in school is only useful at school, while the language learned in other contexts is only useful in those settings. This is, of course, not the case. Think of the way each of us uses language in our daily lives—and the incredible ways we mix language resources across contexts depending on the message and the audience. In the introductory example in this section, we see Michael make use of language learned in other settings to communicate his understanding: "I'd say now that we have, like, the Juan Crow laws. . . . They're doin' the same damn sh . . . stuff." His classmate, Janie, then works to incorporate this idea into the written text that they will use as fodder in the debate. In sum, language use is flexible and this reality should be visible in how we teach.

Binary 2. All language is social language. "School language," in particular, is used for social action in schools. Therefore, it is particularly confusing when we refer to outside-of-school language as "social language," implying that the language learned in schools is somehow the opposite. We combine this functional approach to language with a *sociolinguistic* one to argue that using language in classrooms—or engaging in academic languaging (Swain & Lapkin, 1998; Swain, 2006, 2010)—serves a few purposes. On the one hand, it is a functional resource for communicating content. On the other hand, language can be used for enacting or resisting identities that indicate membership in academic communities (Duff, 2010; Lemke, 2002). From this perspective, students are viewed as social actors who can choose or resist the use of academic language as a means of negotiating membership in both the academic community in the classroom and beyond it. In Ms. Morris's classroom, students enact academic identities using both the language of text and the language they have learned in other settings. Janie also enacts an additional identity often expressed through school language—civil rights advocate: "I'd say that 'As much as things change they stay the same: Today, in the South, we have laws that discriminate against other people, like Latinos. These laws and policies need to change to make society more fair.'"

Of course, this view of language as a tool for social action isn't restricted to the middle grades. In Ms. Foster-Yu's 1st-grade classroom, students are using language as social actors too. Her students work in small groups using math manipulatives (in this case, plastic bears) to make visible the process of addition. The students work together, making this a collaborative reasoning activity in which they must negotiate understanding.

Bowen: I mean, I think it's supposed to be, supposed to be adding.
Geraldo: Adding? You mean put together?

Monica: Right, so let's do this together, I can count the bears. We had three and then two came. So, that's five.
Bowen: Let's draw how we got it. Should I do the bears or make Xs? I think the bears.
Geraldo: But, then we need to show the . . . um . . . the. . . .
Monica: The expression? [begins writing] So . . . it's like . . . gonna be. . . .
Geraldo: Put the plus [pointing] and the equals [pointing].

In this example, we see that using the language typically taught in math classrooms is a social activity (e.g., asking for clarification, collectively rechecking their solution, making sure to show their work). But, as they worked together, Monica, Geraldo, and Bowen are engaged in the kind of talk that we would expect to see in other settings too—perhaps on the playground (e.g., use of "gonna be," pointing, finishing each other's sentences). These examples show that language is always social in nature, a communicative resource for collective action in and out of school.

Planning for Action for Educators

Tips for Language Instruction That Promote Social Interactions for Learning and Avoid Binaries

- Use participation formats that involve working with peers to produce language, whether to have a discussion or to write collaboratively.
- Offer students the opportunity to learn and use language for authentic social purposes, like communicating with a particular audience or to solve a problem of importance to students.
- Make language learning engaging through activities that offer students the chance to puzzle out and to play with language (e.g., www.ioling.org).
- Emphasize how all language is useful and important for communication and participation in social communities and for collective action in and out of school.

In Ms. Morris's classroom, these conditions were present. We see her students frequently working in small groups to produce text and talk for authentic purposes that run the gamut from participating in a debate to expressing their thoughts to authentic audiences outside the classroom. For example, students were also asked to write a Wikipedia entry that exposed the injustices of Jim Crow Laws for the general public, including other social studies students. In another assignment, they were asked to produce a short podcast to serve as an informational resource about the history of these laws for their peers. In these moments, students were invited to use all language resources—those learned at school and in other settings—to make meaning, further underscoring the value of all language resources.

A CONTINUUM PERSPECTIVE TO BEGIN DISMANTLING LANGUAGE HIERARCHIES

The work of dismantling language hierarchies begins with creating classrooms where students are using, on a daily basis, the full range of linguistic resources available to them for communication. We offer the analogy of a continuum and suggest that supporting students in drawing from this continuum offers a necessary antidote to the common practice of reifying linguistic hierarchies in classrooms through the explicit exclusion of home language resources. Next, we examine what this means for instruction.

What Does This Mean for Teaching?

Becoming an Advocate for and Model of Language Fluidity. First, educators must become models and advocates of language fluidity. This entails not only inviting our students to access and to use their broader language resources (Baker-Bell, 2020a; Martínez & Mejía, 2020; Townsend & Lapp, 2010; Uccelli et al., 2020), but also demonstrating these dynamic language practices for our students.

For educators, this often requires a significant shift in our assumptions about language and the role of language instruction—what Kumashiro (2001, 2015) called "unlearning." In our own research, we have documented the beliefs about language that teachers often carry into the classroom, such as viewing English monolingualism as the standard and proficiency in standardized language as the overarching goal of instruction (Heineke & Neugebauer, 2018; Neugebauer & Heineke, 2020a). For many of us, examining how these pervasive ideologies shape our beliefs about our own and our students' language skills is a necessary first step before being able to engage in practices that support linguistic fluidity (Milner, 2007b). The reflective activity at the start of this chapter offers an opportunity to begin this self-examination.

We encourage educators to listen differently to the language used in the classroom—seeking to hear and to understand, rather than to provide feedback or correction. Indeed, Paris and Alim (2017), Paris (2016), and others (Deroo & Ponzio, 2021) have highlighted how it is the listener, not the speaker, who must change how they view the language of the classroom to address the dominance of language hierarchies and monolingual ideologies. We should also be aware that linguistic hierarchies are baked into the curriculum in multiple ways, including in the texts that we select for teaching or that comprise the curricular cannon. We encourage educators and administrators to instead choose texts that highlight linguistic fluidity and to unpack with students how these texts can serve as models of skilled writing (Uccelli et al., 2020; Phillips Galloway & Uccelli, 2019).

Providing Instruction to Support Linguistic Fluidity. Becoming a fluid user of language naturally entails learning new language at the word, sentence, and discourse levels as well as fostering metalinguistic awareness of language practices in context (Nagy & Townsend, 2012; Uccelli et al., 2020). This instruction, instead of focusing on rules for "appropriate" language use, emphasizes language as a resource for communication (McClain et al., 2021). In bell hooks's *Homemade Love* (hooks, 2017), the main character uses evocative, but still child-friendly, language to describe the terms of endearment she is called:

> My Mama calls me
> girlpie.
> Her sweet
> sweet.
> Daddy's honey bun
> Chocolate Dew Drop.

This text used skillfully as a model text invites students to share the names—in English or in a language other than English—used by their families to show that they love them. The range of syntactic structures: "My Mama calls . . . Daddy's" to show ownership are easily replicable in students' own writing and speaking.

Viewing Language Learning (and Language Change) as a Collective Effort. We each bring unique linguistic resources to the classroom. Thus, the work of creating instruction that promotes language fluidity must acknowledge that we are learning from each other. Classrooms must become places of linguistic curiosity, where students and teachers together investigate how language acquired in an array of settings can support communication and learning. As these examples suggest, focusing on the collective work of teachers and students to produce and sharpen language fosters classrooms that are inclusive of students' linguistic resources and allows immediate participation of all students in classroom learning. In addition, language is created in community—and can be changed through social interaction. These three approaches to dismantling language hierarchies guide this volume, as they are necessary for creating equitable language learning environments.

PLANNING FOR ACTION FOR EDUCATORS

Tips for a Continuum Approach to Language Instruction

Here we summarize some key understandings that, when embraced in instruction, support us in dismantling language hierarchies and dichotomous views of language:

- Model language fluidity and invite students to move between all language resources to best communicate thinking.
- Teach language at the word, sentence, and discourse levels to give students a broader range of linguistic options.
- Make language learning collective and emphasize that language can always be changed by members of our classroom community.

Ms. Morris, for example, moved between a host of languages and registers and gave students the chance to do this also. Her lessons were often focused not on words, but on ways of expressing thinking at the sentence-level—a technique that left students with richer applied knowledge of the language they were learning. Finally, her focus on learning language from and with students, and incorporating these resources into her own repertoire, demonstrated the ever-changing nature of the classroom's language community.

CLOSING THOUGHTS ON PROMOTING A CONTINUUM PERSPECTIVE

We have addressed how to become an advocate for language fluidity by questioning language assumptions and listening to the voices of students and the myriad ways they communicate. In the next section of this book, we focus on how language-awareness inquiry routines can draw attention to varied features of language (discourse, vocabulary, and syntax) to support linguistic fluidity.

CHAPTER 3 CLOSING REFLECTION

Now that you have read some classroom examples and learned more about how language use in classrooms can draw on students' entire linguistic repertoires, consider again your response to the initial reflection prompt. How do you or how will you create space in your classroom for students' linguistic resources?

Part II

IN THE CLASSROOM: PRACTICES THAT SUPPORT LINGUISTIC FLUIDITY

Language Beyond Words

> **CONCEPTIONS THAT PROMOTE EQUITABLE LANGUAGE TEACHING**
>
> Language teaching is not about teaching individual words. It is about supporting critical and intentional linguistic fluidity.

Ms. Albertson is a White math educator from Chicago, who stated that she was early in her journey as a critical teacher of language. She knows she must teach her students to access the vocabulary in texts but remains uncertain about what additional features of language she might teach and how to teach these in ways that promote students' ability to adeptly move between language mastered in settings they inhabit both in and out of school. We first met and observed Ms. Albertson and her students in the fall of the school year. In her 7th-grade class, Ms. Albertson introduced a math problem. She wanted to make sure her students could manipulate decimals and fractions, connect math principles to math procedures, and, equally important, she wanted her students to understand that you can arrive at the same solution through different math calculations. She developed the following problem and displayed it on her blackboard:

A coach took his team out for lunch after a basketball game. 2 people each ate .12 of a pizza, 3 people each ate .38 of a pizza. 7 people each ate ¾ of a pizza and the coach had 25/50 of a pizza. What is the least amount of whole pizzas the coach has to buy?

When we talked with Ms. Albertson about the language she saw as critical to engaging with the day's lesson and how she would draw students' attention to language common to math, she explained the challenges of her content area's vocabulary: Her students needed to understand terminology like "proportions," "fractions," and "rounding up." She knew she wanted to start her lesson by reminding students of the definition of the least common denominator—the lowest possible common multiple of the denominators for a set of fractions. However, she also wondered how she might integrate language instruction into her lesson in ways that promote knowledge building and linguistic equity in her classroom. She wanted to do more than just teach content-specific vocabulary.

Many of Ms. Albertson's students belong to communities traditionally excluded from the community of mathematicians (a field dominated by White males): girls, students of color, students who speak a language other than English at home, and students from under-resourced neighborhoods. Ms. Albertson wanted all of her students to see themselves as members of the math community, mathematicians in their own right, able to make their thinking around problem solving visible and knowable by others. She also wanted to create a context that mirrored the authentic ways that math is taken up by mathematicians—acknowledging that there are multiple ways to solve a single problem and these solutions are negotiated among problem solvers using all of their resources. In sum, she wanted to see her students mathematizing—making sense of what was taking place in a word problem in authentic ways before jumping to solve it. She wondered: *How do I teach language to achieve these goals instead of just teaching vocabulary?*

CHAPTER 4 REFLECTION

Take a moment to think about how you teach language or how you have seen it taught. Beyond vocabulary, what aspects of language are critical to the content you teach? How are groups of words put together in meaningful ways in your content area? How does the intended message or communicative purpose influence the language used (e.g., how does the language in Ms. Albertson's math problem differ from the first few paragraphs of a history textbook)? What language use might be marginalizing or excluding for some students in your class and why? How might you advise Ms. Albertson?

Like many teachers, Ms. Albertson could easily identify vocabulary as an area of language teaching that promotes her students' access to the content in her class. The majority of teachers we have worked with, when asked to describe the ways they focus on language in their classrooms, mention "discipline-specific vocabulary," "tier 3 words," or "terminology of the content." For many, language instruction is synonymous with subject-specific vocabulary. This focus cuts across grade levels (Neugebauer & Heineke, 2020b; Heineke & Neugebauer, 2018).

In this chapter, we address multiple elements of language that impact meaning-making and explore how vocabulary is an integral, but not singular, aspect of language instruction. Viewing language as synonymous with vocabulary can limit equitable language teaching, efficacious content learning, and student voice. Instead, equitable language teaching is made possible through language-awareness inquiry routines that ask questions about how communities (e.g., mathematicians) communicate knowledge and information, investigating how words are used, linked, and organized for a particular purpose and audience. Instruction on the language of a particular community (e.g., mathematicians, historians, cinephiles, musicians) need not exclude students' existing language resources. On the contrary, these resources are central to developing linguistic fluidity where students learn to critically and intentionally draw from language used across spaces and communities they inhabit. Thoughtfully selecting language to teach can facilitate alignment with school standards, the use of research-based practices, and simultaneously support student critique, empowerment, and transformation. In this chapter, we describe how to develop language-awareness inquiry routine prompts and select fruitful language features for equitable language instruction.

LANGUAGE: THE WHOLE IS MORE THAN THE SUM OF ITS PARTS

Ms. Albertson wanted to know how to teach language that would support students' math problem solving and thinking, instead of just teaching vocabulary. To begin to answer this question, it helps to highlight constituent parts of language: *vocabulary*—the words used, *syntax*—how we link words together, and *discourse*—language structures that support a particular purpose in a specific context, such as legal discourse in a courtroom. These features are key aspects of language teaching and facilitate reflection and analysis of language use: vocabulary, syntax, and discourse provide language to talk about language, or metalanguage. However, language planning and teaching should begin with a focus on how language supports students in making sense of knowledge and, equally important, how it serves to maintain or disrupt existing structures of power and authority.

Ms. Albertson wanted students to be able to solve the word problem on the board, but more importantly she wanted to support students' knowledge about math learning broadly so that they could see themselves as members of a mathematics community. Ms. Albertson wanted her students to be able to: (a) move back and forth between numbers, symbols, and prose, (b) understand how to solve problems in multiple ways to arrive at the correct answer as part of authentic participation in the mathematics community, and (c) to empower students to use all of their cultural and linguistic resources to make meaning from this word problem in ways that challenge traditional exclusionary forces that marginalize some students.

Ms. Albertson cannot address all of these aims successfully in a single lesson. Instead, she considered how her lessons across the unit might work together. For each class, Ms. Albertson used the steps listed as follows to plan and engage in content-directed iterative questioning that draws students' attention to the power of language and flexible linguistic choices at their disposal:

Step 1. She considered how her questions would need to push students to consider how language inscribes power, and ways to bolster their own empowerment. Specifically, she asked herself: *What prompts will help students critique how mathematicians communicate knowledge in particular ways? What prompts will highlight the ways in which power is instantiated and maintained in math?*

Step 2. She considered how the math community prescribes specific language structures and features, and how her questions might help students reflect on this language. Specifically, she asked herself: *What prompts will improve students' ability to reflect on and manipulate the structural features of language in math communities? What prompts will uncover linguistic injustice and/or the power of linguistic fluidity?*

Step 3. She considered the discourse, vocabulary, and syntax that support meaning-making in math communities. Specifically, she asked herself: *What prompts will facilitate attention to the language that characterizes math meaning-making (e.g., language which prescribes a particular organization and sequence in which knowledge is disseminated)? What prompts will highlight language that links ideas in particular ways? What prompts will get students to explore words and terms that encapsulate critical ideas or help deliver those critical ideas?*

In the sections that follow, we examine each of these critical steps for developing powerful language awareness inquiry routine prompts to understand how these prompts can support critical and empowering language use, consumption, fluidity, and content learning.

Step 1: Prompts to Critique Knowledge and Power

In every community, there are rules about participation and conventions for how people should participate and disseminate information. In the community of mathematicians, precise and explicit language is highly valued. Mathematicians rarely use language for the purpose of evoking strong feelings or for expressing emotion, unlike in a literary community, where stimulating strong feelings shows one's talent and craft. Participation in these communities involves playing the part of an active and included member through the use of particular language patterns that validate and affirm the way knowledge is enacted in that specific community.

Because we see language as not just about what is said but about "acting" or "playing" in ways that are consistent with participation rules and conventions of a particular community, we refer to this aspect of language use as *scripts.* We use the term scripts to capture how language patterns, conventions, rules, and ways of disseminating and acting upon information are set by specific communities. Scripts are similar to concepts described by Gee (2012; 1996) that frame language as the enactment of social and cultural identities and perspectives. Identifying these scripts can support students in enacting and consuming language for the purpose of critiquing the ways they preserve certain ways of knowing and belonging associated with specific communities and thus serve as a transformational activity.

Scripts involve enacting a particular identity and using language associated with that perspective and way of being and knowing. The most common scripts in school are those associated with academic disciplines. Written or spoken, these scripts are influenced by the ways knowledge is constructed and enacted in a given field (Shanahan & Shanahan, 2008). Disciplines disseminate knowledge in ways that are specialized (e.g., historians read and write arguments with evidence, mathematicians read and write for precision). As a result, discipline-specific scripts that prescribe how to enact and disseminate knowledge are often exclusionary.

For example, a common script for historians centers on historical analysis in which they explore the complexity of historical events and unique perspectives of different actors. A student who is not keyed into this script or way of enacting historical knowledge will read a set of primary source letters (e.g., letters to the Spanish king by conquistadors who destroyed the Aztecs' capital) and focus exclusively on facts about dates or timelines (e.g., the conquistadors arrived in Mexico in 1519) but may not focus on the unique language of each letter writer (e.g., Bernal Dias del Castillo) and the linguistic features that reveal the cultural and religious assumptions (e.g., "their [the Aztecs] diabolical and cursed lewdness") and perspectives of the letter writer that influence their perceptions of the causes and outcomes of events (Diaz, 1963). The unique scripts of the disciplines provide a critical opportunity in instruction to question and probe how disciplinary ways of disseminating information maintain power and privilege. Language-awareness inquiry routine prompts should interrogate these scripts to support students in consuming and critiquing these ways of communicating and belonging to a community.

When planning her lesson, using the word problem on the board to talk about solving the same math problem in different ways, Ms. Albertson attended to disciplinary scripts enacted by math communities. Specifically, she integrated the following prompts into the lesson: "How do we decide when/if we want to use math language? Can I say this same thing using other words—not necessarily mathematical language? Why do you think mathematicians use certain language?"

When she used these prompts with her students, they noticed that certain aspects of mathematical language were helpful in concisely expressing an idea. As students used their existing linguistic resources—in English and in other languages—to explain the word problem, they noticed that there was great utility in having to move between different types of languages and scripts. We often have language already that can help us express the precise mathematical terms used (e.g., "Let's put all those together" versus "Sum all components"). Ms. Albertson's questions about why mathematical language came into being guided the conversation to a discussion that concluded with a twofold answer: Mathematical language offers functional components that are helpful for concisely and precisely communicating thinking to members of the math community, *and* using this language serves to create a sense of in-group membership that excludes other individuals and ways of thinking beyond those that traditionally dominate in mathematics.

This discussion problematized the relationship between language and power, with prompts like "Can we claim this language as our own? If so, how?" In response, students realized that they wanted to take up some aspects of math's disciplinary script and reject others. For example, Mariana argued that math scripts seemed to position language as neutral but, as she explained, "Math talk is not just numbers. It is also about who is in or out, because using it you are a 'winner' or a 'loser.' You are like a good student or not a good student." Another student said she wanted more "honest" math scripts that showed "math is being done for a reason." As a class, they decided that they wanted to disrupt the idea of math as neutral and come up with a project that would help them apply the lesson goals around multiple solutions by using a variety of linguistic resources to advocate for a personal cause. They examined the school schedule to calculate how more time could be allocated to student special interest clubs, and used math language such as first, second, and third to illustrate their step-by-step solution for how more time would be feasible given the current schedule. Students also integrated their personal flare throughout their presentation language, such as expressing their enthusiasm and passion for special interest groups, "They make my week!" The whole class also convinced Ms. Albertson that there should be no more math problems that focus on pizza! These prompts and the discussion that ensued supported students in identifying and critiquing linguistic features of the math community and equally important gave them tools for creatively using language for their own goals.

Step 2: Prompts for Reflection on Language

Language-awareness inquiry routines also dissect and parse linguistic choices and uses in disciplinary scripts. Metalinguistic prompts help students reflect on and manipulate the structural features of language. Ms. Albertson's content goal to use multiple methods for solving the same problem was rooted in research that found teaching multiple methods for the same solution increases students' math achievement (Star et al., 2016). To meet this goal, Ms. Albertson wanted to get students in the habit of considering how words, symbols, and prose indicate what to do with a particular math challenge and how to do it. Ms. Albertson encouraged a line of thinking around language choices and features with the prompts: "What words tell me what to do and how to do it? Can I solve this more than one way? And what language signals this?" These prompts encourage attention to the ways language can cue students into specific purposes and meaning-making strategies.

In math scripts, a focus on precision of language is paramount (e.g., the difference between "a" and "the" can change the procedure used!) (Shanahan & Shanahan, 2008). These prompts draw students' attention to approaches useful for mathematical meaning-making around multiple method solutions. Equally important, these prompts highlight for students that language can be organized and subsequently interpreted in different ways ("'Two people each ate .12 of a pizza' means I should have two times .12 of a pizza or I should add .12 of a pizza and .12 of a pizza"). Metalinguistic prompts guide students in better understanding how knowledge is constructed and disseminated in the language of math communities. These language awareness inquiry routine questions are part of a social process of showing students ways to draw meaning in math, and how careful attention to language can support disciplinary meaning-making.

Metalinguistic prompts about the disciplinary script will help guide subsequent questions on other language features (i.e., discourse, vocabulary, and syntax). In Figure 4.1 we provide the language-awareness inquiry routine lesson planning template with the planned prompts for Ms. Albertson's math class. We describe how to develop these specific prompts (i.e., discourse, vocabulary, and syntax) in the next section. The transformational and metalinguistic prompts about the disciplinary script anchor and drive questions about specific language features that characterize the way information is disseminated and meaning is made in the disciplines. For example, prompts like, "What words tell me what to do and how to do it?" will make mathematical vocabulary such as "compare," "method," and "procedure" particularly relevant and worth exploring. A review of these constituent features will also support students' analysis of whether they feel they can claim this language as their own. The pedagogical intention is that these questions about specific language features (vocabulary, syntax, and discourse) are aligned with supporting students in answering larger metalinguistic and transformational questions.

When language awareness inquiry routines are used across subject area classrooms, they bolster students' ability to see language choices as connected to distinctive purposes. For example, across multiple lessons, Ms. Albertson made several cross-disciplinary connections about the role of language in meaning-making. To conclude one lesson, she asked her students to think of another example of how they "read language and thought in two ways" outside of her classroom. Arav raised his hand and referenced their reading the day before of *The Road Not Taken,* by Robert Frost (Frost et al., 1991). He explained, "Yaass! Seriously, like, no cap, I read it and like then I read it again, and again, and it was totally different, but the words were the same!" Arav was amazed that he had been able to interpret the same poem, with the same words, in two ways.

Figure 4.1. Ms. Albertson's Planning

	Language Awareness Inquiry Prompts	
Language System Element	**Metalinguistic Prompts**	**Transformational Prompts**
Math Script	What words tell me what to do and how to do it? Can I solve this more than one way? What language signals this?	How do we decide when/if we want to use disciplinary language? Can we claim this language as our own? If so, how?
Discourse	Can I retrace my steps by rereading the problem again for specific language on order and sequencing?	
Vocabulary	What do common denominator, like terms, improper fraction, sum, compare, method, and procedure mean in this context?	
Syntax	How and when should we use: "I estimated __________ *but* calculation revealed __________" or "First I calculated using __________ then I recalculated using ______" to describe our math process?	

Ms. Albertson has team planning meetings with the 7th grade English teacher, Mr. Ebony, a Black man also originally from Chicago. They had previously discussed how they would both emphasize attention to language synergistically across their two content area classes. Ms. Albertson knew that Mr. Ebony had worked with his students on exploring the poem *The Road Not Taken,* contrasting the common interpretation of this poem as inspirational and about the importance of taking your own path, with a more subversive and pessimistic message about loss and doubt in life decisions. She asked Arav to say more, using a specific example from the text of what he meant. He explained that "in one line he [the author] talks about the road going different ways and he goes on one and I was like 'Wow, he is real strong,' but then I read it again and again, like he says the word 'I' twice that makes it sound like he is all choked up, like . . . 'wah wah I . . . I . . . I.' He is not confident after all."

Ms. Albertson and Mr. Ebony are each supporting students in attending to language in ways that promote distinct disciplinary purposes. Ms. Albertson used language-awareness inquiry routines that pushed students to focus on how attention to language can signal different mathematical procedures and how rereading and retracing is essential for catching language features that support meaning-making in math. Mr. Ebony focused his lesson on *The Road Not Taken* on language-awareness inquiry routine prompts that highlighted the disciplinary scripts of literature, where he drew attention to language that was figurative or had multiple meanings (e.g., "How is feeling or emotion conveyed in the author's language? What language signals emotion?"). Together, these teachers were engaging in language-awareness inquiry routines that honed teacher and students' ability to reflect on disciplinary scripts in ways that empower dissection and critique, deepen learning, and linguistic fluidity. By being explicit about how meaning-making is arrived at through language choices, Ms. Albertson and Mr. Ebony both showcased for students how language features reveal sensemaking important to specific disciplinary communities.

Language-awareness inquiry routines should highlight how to "play" or take up meaning-making in a particular disciplinary community to support students in being able to flexibly and critically consume and evaluate scripts for a variety of purposes, and in so doing, facilitate their own intentional language choices (Gee, 2012). In the following text box, we show Ms. Albertson's preplanned transformational and metalinguistic questions and approach to this lesson.

PLANNING FOR ACTION FOR THE CLASSROOM

Disciplinary Script Tips

Ms. Albertson framed her lesson around:
Transformational Language-Awareness Inquiry Prompts

- How do we decide when/if we want to use disciplinary language?
- Can we claim this language as our own? If so, how?

Metalinguistic Language-Awareness Inquiry Prompts

- What words tell me what to do and how to do it?
- Can I solve this more than one way? What language signals this?

Begin with these prompts as the routine you use for multiple classes with similar word problems, and use these prompts to guide the discourse, syntax, and vocabulary you attend to.

To demonstrate how these prompts may be taken up across classrooms, we provide the lesson planning template for a group of teachers who all teach 7th grade in Figure 4.2. While, the examples here focus on disciplinary scripts, we encourage readers to see scripts as an analytic tool that opens the door for exploring many language communities beyond those most accepted in school. This chart shows language-awareness inquiry routines can

Figure 4.2. Language-Awareness Inquiry Prompt Planning Across Content Area Classrooms

	Math Solving Using Multiple Methods (Chapter 4)		Science Reviewing a Biology Text (Chapter 5)	
Language System Element	**Metalinguistic Prompts**	**Transformational Prompts**	**Metalinguistic Prompts**	**Transformational Prompts**
Scripts	What words tell me what to do and how to do it? Can I solve this more than one way? What language signals this?	How do we decide when/ if we want to use disciplinary language? Can we claim this language as our own? If so, how?	How and why do snakes change form? What scientific language provides clues for why they change form?	Science focuses, through language choices, on processes and evidence. Does this focus exclude some knowledge over others? What evidence from the world is valued?
Discourse	Can I retrace my steps by rereading the problem again for specific language on order and sequencing?		What language signals a cause-and-effect relationship?	
Vocabulary	What do common denominator, like terms, improper fraction, sum, compare, method, and procedure mean in this context?		This passage is focused on different snakes' survival—the snakes' ability to live and continuing living even when faced with challenges from the natural world—what are some vocabulary terms that address what contributes to a snake's survival or benefits a snake's survival? (Examples: reproduce, adapt, camouflage)	
Syntax	How and when should we use: "I estimated __________ *but* calculation revealed ___________" or "First I calculated using __________ then I recalculated using ______" to describe our math process?		How does this author use diverse sentence starters? What does this linguistic diversity do for communicating the authors' ideas ("In this environment"; "on a forest floor").	

ELA Analyzing *Roll of Thunder, Hear My Cry* (Chapter 6)		Social Studies Debating Vaccination (Chapter 5)	
Metalinguistic Prompts	**Transformational Prompts**	**Metalinguistic Prompts**	**Transformational Prompts**
How is the theme of injustice and power shown in the idioms and language used in this chapter?	How does the language or dialect in this work influence how we understand the experience of protagonist?	What language helps us persuade and make an argument?	Does certain language persuade when it comes to debate? Why? Should it?
How is the language of the teachers different than the language of the children? How is authority being communicated in these different ways?		What types of evidence helps me substantiate my argument and what language helps me do that?	
What do these words tell us about the characters? "jammed" "thrust" "maverick" "imprisoned freedom" "indignant anger/ indignation"		Words to highlight and define: vaccination, individual rights, public good, outweigh, privilege	
How does the use of "ain't" influence how we make meaning of these sentences?: "You *ain't* never had to live in nobody's place but your own." "Yes, *ain't* that something?"		How and in what ways do these sentence starters help us persuade our peers? "He argues____ however, I argue _______" "Evidence to support—is" "Furthermore, we should not _______ because. . . ."	

be used flexibly across a variety of contexts with different content goals and that represent different disciplinary communities. Language-awareness inquiry routines provide a framework for supporting content-driven exchanges but do not prescribe specific language features teachers must attend to. Teachers can draw from the steps provided here to determine the language they should focus on in their specific content area, grade level, and classroom community. The specific prompts vary, but the approach to equitable language teaching stays constant.

Step 3: Prompts to Explore Language Features

We use the term *discourse* to refer to linguistic structures beyond the sentence level. These structures create an organizational framework for how messages are delivered. Discourse has been defined by linguists Michael Halliday and Ruqaiya Hasan (1990) as language that is both more than a single sentence and grounded in a particular context. This definition of discourse highlights the linguistic unit (i.e., larger than a sentence) and emphasizes the context in which a message is situated, that is, the person speaking, listening, and the "when and where" of the language event that influences the features of the language used.

We encourage teachers in their work with students to identify discourse organizational structures as they help students more easily dissect the meaning of text and identify language that allows an author to weave together information in a way that communicates ideas for a specific purpose. For example, a world history passage about the Bubonic plague might be organized in terms of a "cause and effect" discourse, where the passage describes how and where the disease spread and evidence to support why it spread:

> Most experts believed the (Bubonic Plague) was *caused* by a germ called *Yersinia pestis.* In 2011, scientists studying centuries-old skeletons *confirmed* that the experts were right about this germ. The germ lived in the bodies of fleas that attached themselves to rats. In the 1300s, rats were a part of everyday life in the cities and villages of Europe. They lived in streets and alleys. They lived in people's homes. Infected fleas that bit people passed the disease on to them. People could also catch the disease by coming in close contact with someone who had already fallen ill. (Kucan & Palincsar, 2013)

In this paragraph, the language choices (such as the use of "caused" and "confirmed" to highlight the internal structure related to identifying a problem and its causes) as well as language about who is identifying the problem ("experts believed" and "scientists studying") signal the frame of this text. That is, they reflect a discourse of cause and effect and evidence to support such a causal relationship, common to meaning-making in history. Understanding the discourse of the text is essential for students as they learn to tease out what language to attend to and how disciplinary scripts show how communities disseminate knowledge through specific language structures.

Other discourse text structures or frames common in school include (Buehl, 2011; Jones et al., 1987):

- Problem/solution text frame: a problem needs solving
- Cause and effect text frame: certain conditions lead to certain results
- Compare and contrast text frame: certain things are similar or different
- Goal/action/outcome text frame: someone is doing something for specific reasons
- Concept/definition text frame: a concept needs to be understood
- Proposition/support text frame: a viewpoint is being argued and supported

If a student approached the entirety of the passage provided on the Bubonic plague as a concept definition frame, they might focus on terms like Bubonic plague or dates, but not track the progression of the text from disease spread to containing the disease. They might miss how the language used in the text such as "deduced" or "they hypothesized" or "confirmed" is intended to help students to think like a historian about how events serve as catalysts for other events and reactions and how we verify a causal historical argument (Shanahan & Shanahan, 2008; Moje, 2015). Understanding the discourse of a given text helps facilitate a synthesis of the text and prevents it from feeling like a sea of details as opposed to a coherent structure articulated through language that cues the reader to a specific text frame.

Alternatively, a biology textbook with a chapter on bacteria would more commonly adopt a concept/definition discourse text frame, with the chapter providing terms related to bacteria (e.g., living organisms, eukaryotes, prokaryotes, adaptation), a description of what they look like and where they live, as well as examples of bacteria (e.g., *Yersinia pestis* is the bacteria that caused Bubonic plague). For example:

> Bacteria are organisms that consist of a single, prokaryotic cell. Bacteria are the only prokaryotes (cells with no nuclei). All other life forms on Earth are eukaryotes. Bacterial cells have a cell membrane that is surrounded by a tough cell wall.

The disciplinary script dictates the discourse or frame of the message, which sets a structure for how ideas will be linked (syntax) and the words that signal the purpose and deliver the content (vocabulary). Understanding and explicitly highlighting discourse with language-awareness inquiry routine prompts support students in developing metalinguistic skills, in that they are better able to reflect on and access these internal structures.

Focusing on text discourse structures should not prescribe how students talk as they build subject-specific knowledge. For example, in Ms. Albertson's classroom, students engage in discussions in sync with the disciplinary script and discourse of math sensemaking but use language resources beyond those provided by their teacher or the lesson. Ms. Albertson asked the class whether they could revisit the coach's problem about how many pizzas he needed to buy again, this time looking for specific language on sequencing. Jamie turned to his table partner, Juanita, and described that he initially got 7.13, but after rereading he explained "Oh oh . . . no seas codo, coach" and tapped his elbow smiling, exclaiming "whole pizzas!" Jamie is engaging with the prompt focused on rereading for language cues and is taking up the problem/solution text frame of attending closely to language that signals the type of solution requested, i.e., a final whole number. However, he is also drawing on his varied language resources to construct meaning. Specifically, he jokingly used the expression "no seas codo!", "don't be stingy!" in Spanish, which is typically accompanied by the gesture of tapping your elbow, to be playful with Juanita that if the coach bought 7.13 of a pizza he would be miserly; he has to buy the full pizza, not a couple of extra slices.

When Jamie and Juanita are chosen to describe their procedures for solving the problem to the whole class, they explicitly used language like "first," "second," and "next" to describe their steps, engaging a discourse Ms. Albertson has taught them that helps their peers make meaning of their approach to the problem. The discourse or internal structure of their remarks followed a step-by-step description of each stage of their mathematical procedures, an idea Ms. Albertson has emphasized in her questions around specific language on order and sequencing. They carefully demonstrated for their peers language that helped them decide to use multiplication when the word "each" was used, and they explained that "*whole* pizzas reminds you that you have to round up to 8." In their presentation, they used language that was explicit for math reasoning so that they could scaffold the learning of their peers, a linguistically diverse crowd. Jamie and Juanita were able to assess the context and audience and assess the effectiveness of a particular language choice for communicating a specific math procedure.

Ms. Albertson used her observation of Jamie and Juanita's exchange as an opportunity to unpack her preplanned transformative prompts on how the discourse of math prescribes the ways in which power is instantiated and maintained in disciplinary scripts. "*How do we decide when/if we want to use disciplinary language? Can we claim this language as our own? If so, how?*" In the following text box, we show Ms. Albertson's preplanned discourse questions and approach to this lesson.

Planning for Action for the Classroom

Discourse Tips

Language-Awareness Inquiry Prompts for discourse

- Can I retrace my steps by rereading the problem again for specific language on order and sequencing?

Begin with these prompts as the routine you use for multiple classes with similar word problems, and use these prompts to guide the syntax, and vocabulary you attend to.

Ms. Albertson's final steps in preparing her lesson focused on developing prompts to help students explore words that capture or present critical ideas as well as prompts to highlight language that links ideas. At the beginning of this chapter, Ms. Albertson explained that she felt the most confident in her ability to choose words that would support the lesson content. Indeed, well-documented is the strong, positive, and longitudinal impact of vocabulary on students' ability to comprehend complex academic texts (Elleman et al., 2009; Ouellette, 2006) and by extension succeed in school (Corson, 1997; García, 1991; Snow & Kim, 2007). So, it stands to reason that vocabulary would be an important focus of instruction for Ms. Albertson, and discipline-specific vocabulary is the most intuitive aspect of language teaching (Nagy & Townsend, 2012). However, talking about and consuming disciplinary content requires that students learn words beyond just subject-specific terms, and an equity-focused approach entails a more critical lens for selecting words that will be the focus of instruction.

Vocabulary words are typically broken up into distinct categories. One type is commonly referred to as "tier 3," "content-specific," or "discipline-specific" words. Content-specific words are the most common focus of language and disciplinary instruction. Another categorical distinction is "tier 2" words, also referred to as "all-purpose academic" vocabulary, words that help students talk about, read, and write about those content words, which are critical for school learning (Beck et al., 2013; Lesaux et al., 2010; Snow, Lawrence, & White, 2009). Tier 2 or "all-purpose academic" words often represent new labels for concepts students already know and understand (e.g., sum, calculate, compare). By contrast, content-specific vocabulary requires students to learn new concepts while also learning new labels (e.g., photosynthesis, tangent, simile, etc.) (Beck et al., 2013). Teaching these two types of vocabulary usually goes hand in hand, in that talking about content-specific words often obliges the use of all-purpose academic words as well (Beck et al., 2013). These two types of words are often contrasted with more common words like clock, baby, house, sometimes referred to as "tier 1" words, that students often come to school already knowing. While multilingual learners may not yet have learned some tier 1 vocabulary in English, they generally know them in a first language.

But the delineation between words of different categories is never so clear cut in real classrooms or in everyday language use. In advocating for instruction that promotes linguistic fluidity and creates linguistically permeable spaces, we encourage teachers to conceptualize words as falling along a continuum, as opposed to discrete categories. There has been considerable research to show that these vocabulary divisions or categories commonly lead to uncertain use or misapplication of vocabulary strategies (Flanigan & Greenwood, 2007; Snell et al., 2015). Teasing out which words are staunchly discipline-specific and which words are all-purpose can be difficult (e.g., in a first-grade classroom talking about birds, is *predator* a discipline-specific or all-purpose word?). While some words are more likely to be encountered in specific disciplinary contexts (e.g., angle in geometry), we can't rule out other uses of these terms in other settings (e.g., move the painting up, it is at an angle!). Other words are more malleable and can be taken up across disciplinary contexts but carry a distinctive meaning in each setting (e.g., you can *analyze* the poem in English language arts, and *analyze* the numbers in math). Approaching word selection with a focus on having a handful of "discipline-specific" words and "all-purpose" words may not necessarily maximize content learning. Teaching the word *predator* explicitly is critical to content conversations about animal survival, carnivores, and herbivores, and yet it is hard to categorize this word as one or the other type of word. By contrast, eagle (discipline-specific) and approach (all-purpose) are more easily identifiable as these two types of words, but are less critical to the learning of the big ideas of the lesson.

We encourage less attention to "tiers" in favor of focusing on what students need to know to access the disciplinary script, talk about content learning, and understand the content. Ms. Albertson had a difficult time describing the manipulation of fractions and ideas like "least common denominator" without using words like calculate, compare, and sum. Calculate, compare, and sum could be used across contexts, were important to the disciplinary script, and were essential for talking about the different procedures that the students used to solve the math problems in distinctive ways. She knew she had to teach her students accessible definitions of these math terms for the lesson.

Words with more applicability across contexts that support students' discussion of more specialized words are often taught incidentally. Students often learn these words solely in the context of a sentence (Nagy & Townsend, 2012; Lesaux et al., 2010). But such brief exposures to words fail to create a space for all students to engage with words and their meaning. Language-awareness inquiry routines provide opportunities for engaging in direct teaching and evaluating of all words that support content learning. Asking probing questions about these words provides opportunities for students to hear words used multiple times, to hear them contrasted with other words with related meanings, and for teachers to define, model, and critique their use (Beck et al., 2013).

In Ms. Foster-Yu's 1st-grade classroom, she engaged in explicit vocabulary instruction in the course of her language-awareness inquiry routine prompts to address content on linguistic prejudice. In the course of her questioning, she defined prejudice. "This word means that somebody doesn't like another person before they even have met them because of their race or religion! 'Pre-' means before . . . 'Prejudice' means pre-judging someone." She highlighted morphemes (i.e., the smallest unit of meaning in words, such as prefixes, suffixes, and root words) by drawing students' attention to the prefix "pre-." Then she talked about this word in relationship to the words equality and racism. Ms. Foster-Yu engaged in practices that directly addressed the lesson's content. Her instruction incorporated the definition of the word and its parts, provided multiple contexts in which the word could be used, and supported deep processing by comparing and contrasting related words (Baumann et al., 2003; NICHD, 2000; Stahl & Fairbanks, 1986). With her class, Ms. Foster-Yu effectively explored words that are less fluid in their use and specific to their content (e.g., prejudice) as well as words that can be used in other contexts and to deepen understanding of other conceptually related terms (e.g., equal).

If Ms. Albertson applied these same strategies in her math class, she might provide an accessible definition of the word "sum" by saying, "When we sum these numbers, we add them together," as opposed to a textbook definition of sum such as, "A particular aggregate of a total," with the latter definition requiring that students know the word "aggregate." She might provide contextual information about the word by explaining an experience that captured this word, such as, "Last week we summed several fractions, or added them together, to get one fraction that equaled the whole amount." Throughout her lesson she might use this word in a variety of ways such as "summed fractions together," "calculated the sum," or "sum the multiple decimals," using the word with different morphological endings (e.g., different suffixes such as sum*s*, summ*ed*, summ*ing*). In addition, she might ask students how the word sum is different from the word "merge" or "tally," other related words to which students have been exposed. Ms. Albertson might have a Word Wall, a bulletin board with an array of words written out in big letters, that includes all of these words around arithmetic principles helping students to evaluate how a new word relates to words they already know and how these words represent a word network that will grow over time (Fitzgerald et al., 2020).

By acknowledging how a variety of words that may be more or less discipline-specific work together to support the disciplinary script, teachers are able to give students access to the curriculum to help them talk about new ideas and concepts, and to make connections about how concepts are communicated in discipline-specific ways. Language-awareness inquiry routines provide opportunities for students to engage in back-and-forth exchanges where they can authentically use selected words to construct, disseminate, and critique disciplinary knowledge generation and the fluidity of such language across spaces and audiences.

PLANNING FOR ACTION FOR THE CLASSROOM

Vocabulary Tips

1. Choose a handful of words that fall along a fluidity continuum to support content learning, understanding the discourse and disciplinary language, and which facilitate student contributions to language awareness inquiry routine prompts.
2. Words selected should be aligned with your language-awareness inquiry routine aims and thus highlight essential meaning-making.
3. Support vocabulary learning with explicit instruction that includes a) a friendly or accessible definition of the word; b) examples in disciplinary contexts; c) exposure across varied uses and morphological endings; and d) comparing, contrasting, and juxtaposing related words and why a given word serves a purpose.

Ms. Albertson's chosen words included: common denominator, like terms, and improper fraction. To help students talk about these words and respond to her language prompts focused on mathematizing, she also chose to focus on: sum, compare, method, and procedure.

When teaching language, attending to the ways ideas are linked (i.e., their syntax and grammar) is often overlooked, but is critical to meaning-making. For example, the math textbook Ms. Albertson uses contains sentences like: *The division of an integer is performed, however, with the opposite operation as multiplying integers*. This same sentence could be read as, *You can divide an integer the opposite way you multiply an integer*. Instead, this math text begins with the process—dividing an integer. The opposing processes described in the math textbook are linked by the word "however," grammar that deviates from how students might usually speak. Transitions and connectives like "however" that are used in academic texts (Hyland, 2004) can be highlighted in language-awareness inquiry routine prompts, with teachers creating space to discuss how they influence a written sentence, to clarify their meaning, and to relate these language features to the discourse and disciplinary script of the lesson's content area (Uccelli et al., 2015).

Teachers can draw attention to these grammatical markers by showcasing sentence frames that include connectives or transitions for students to use and critique in speaking or writing. For example, Ms. Albertson, might have offered the sentence starter/frame "I estimated ____________ *but* calculation revealed ______________," or "First I calculated using __________ then I recalculated using ______." These sentence frames drive home some of the core language features Ms. Albertson's language-awareness inquiry routine prompts attempt to highlight and are aligned with math research on how student math predictions support mathematical sensemaking and reasoning (Kasmer & Kim, 2012).

While no more complex than the language used in speech, disciplinary-written sentences constitute a challenge to readers who must "unpack" each idea. Typical sentences in subject-area texts frequently contain multiple clauses. For example, this sentence typifies sentence structures used in social studies textbooks: *The queen, who was regarded as the primary ruler, was without the experience needed to lead the fractured country, resulting in low morale and disorganization at all levels of government.* Readers must connect the clause beginning with "who" to "queen" to understand what is being said. The commas, while helpful to a reader familiar with parsing the texts' ideas in this way, may be confusing to readers with little experience reading texts that contain these features.

To give students the tools needed to access and investigate more complex sentences, we find it helpful to model how these sentences can be parsed as part of language-awareness inquiry prompts. This social studies sentence might be rewritten as multiple standalone sentences. Sentence-combining activities, in which students put together or analyze a series of distinct sentences, are a useful classroom practice. These activities are best done collaboratively, allowing students to learn from peers with different amounts of experience navigating disciplinary texts. Students are compelled to explore new grammatical structures, including connectives, as they work to combine or parse sentences. For example, students in Ms. Albertson's class each have another math student in the school they write to (a math pen pal!). The students wrote to their pen pals about multiple ways to solve math problems. Students moved from three sentences such as: "I can calculate the answer in two ways. I can multiply .12 by 2. I can also add .12 and .12," to combined sentences like, "I can calculate .24 by multiplying .12 by 2, or by adding .12 and .12." Sentence combining pushes students to understand grammar in ways that translate to their own writing (Berninger et al., 2010). These grammar activities should be driven by a larger content-learning objective that focuses on dissecting how different types of messages are conveyed.

Planning for Action for the Classroom

Syntax Tips

1. Highlight words that link ideas in writing and speech in a particular disciplinary community.
2. To support linguistic fluidity, provide sentence frames that encourage the use of grammatical structures that support meaning-making in the discipline, and draw students' attention to these language markers and focus on these in your language-awareness inquiry prompts to support metalinguistic and transformative purposes.
3. Support students in seeing the range of grammatical language choices that serve distinct purposes, by engaging in critical sentence-combining activities.

Ms. Albertson provides her students with sentence frames that support their explicit step-by-step discussion of their different solution methods, language common to math meaning-making and for sharing math information with peers during her language-awareness inquiry routine discussions. She has students write in their math journals and engage in sentence-combining activities that support honing their craft in making intentional language choices about how to explicitly communicate information to a particular audience. In subsequent lessons, her language-awareness inquiry prompts contrast different examples of sentence combining and their effect on the reader.

MOVING AWAY FROM VOCABULARY-BASED TEACHING

The ideas presented in this chapter are not about focusing on rules for "appropriate" language use. Instead, they see language as a functional resource for authentic communication and learning (McClain et al., 2021). Language awareness inquiry routines that promote transformation and metalinguistic awareness where students can reflect on the script, discourse, vocabulary, and syntax of a particular language community are essential for creating a critical and intentional linguistically porous space.

These routines focus on developing linguistic fluidity and value the essential role that students' varied linguistic resources can play in developing metalinguistic and transformative thinking about language use, rather than reifying a linguistic standard. For example, Ms. Albertson used the language-awareness inquiry routine prompts listed in her lesson-planning template to talk about how information is disseminated in different ways depending on the purpose and audience. For several weeks, her class had been talking about translating word problems in ways that require students to move between words and math notation to solve a problem. Ms. Albertson was eager to show students how they already move between different linguistic systems, such as the language of texting. She told us she also engaged in this work to fend off student jokes about her as a "Luddite," as they often say they need "Ms. Albertson 2.0, the current model is too old." She had students share some of their text messages the week before, and she selected a couple of useful text examples to showcase the role of linguistic choices in meaning-making and scripts beyond the disciplines. As a class, they dissected several messages to explore how language functions differently depending on the communicative goal, which is influenced by the audience, context, and purpose. Ms. Albertson framed the lesson around answering the larger question: whether and how the language in their text messages might serve math discussions. She used the discourse, vocabulary, and syntax prompts in her planning template (Figure 4.3) to parse what is unique about ways of disseminating information—revealing an underlying script—in Remy and Julia's text message exchange.

> *Remy:* hola sis!
> *Julia:* digame
> *Remy:* go to CPL [Chicago Public Library] for a little. Gina be there.
> *Julia:* asking moms. Its on. See you in 40.
> *Remy:* Mama girl . . . ja, ja.

By using the prompts in Figure 4.3, Ms. Albertson drew students' attention to the use of "hola," a shared first language, and "mama girl" to convey intimacy. She highlighted the use of an acronym to convey in-group knowledge of a place and more efficiently communicate. She questioned the students' morphological choices such as adding an "s" to mom or removing the apostrophe and "s" in "mama's girl" that is consistent with adolescent grammar and the need for less of a workout for the texting thumb.

Ms. Albertson was able to unpack the text message and show how the language in this text exchange involved moving between language systems (e.g., across Spanish and English, recognizing acronyms) and related this back to their work on the word problems and the way we can fluidly move between words, symbols, and ways of talking to solve word problems and also construct meaning in more meaningful ways. She complimented the students' texts, applauding how these messages show their ability to navigate complex context-specific scripts.

Students debated how they might use acronyms productively in two of the word problems from the day before and how the language of math—and its focus on precision—excludes language that might evoke intimacy,

Figure 4.3. Ms. Albertson's Language-Awareness Routine Prompts and Aims for Text Messaging

<table>
<tr><th></th><th colspan="2">Language-Awareness Inquiry Prompts</th></tr>
<tr><th>Language System Element</th><th>Metalinguistic Prompts</th><th>Transformational Prompts</th></tr>
<tr><td>Script</td><td>How does language use in text messages provide a unique space for intimacy?</td><td rowspan="4">Does this language serve math discussions? If so, how?</td></tr>
<tr><td>Discourse</td><td>What language in this text exchange communicates closeness?</td></tr>
<tr><td>Vocabulary</td><td>Remy says "CPL" instead of the Chicago Public Library; does using CPL communicate something beyond its meaning?</td></tr>
<tr><td>Syntax</td><td>Julia says "asking moms" and Remy says "mama girl"; this is a distinctive grammar that removes possessives, what does this use convey and what unique purpose does it serve?</td></tr>
</table>

picking up the conversation from the previous discussion of math as seemingly neutral. In each of her lessons, Ms. Albertson encouraged students to co-construct knowledge using all their linguistic resources and the varied communicative devices at their disposal.

Language is far more than vocabulary. Language has constituent parts that include word, sentence, and discourse structures. These features reflect varied communicative goals related to disciplinary communities and, more broadly, to any community that has agreed upon norms or scripts. Recognizing that language is a resource for authentic communication (McClain et al., 2021) emphasizes why teaching equitably should not be about teaching isolated constituent language parts but instead about engaging in rich language-awareness inquiry routines driven by transformational aims to critically evaluate the relationship between language and power. These routines should be implemented with metalinguistic prompts that parse and uncover the way language functions to communicate particular meaning for a specific audience, context, and purpose with different linguistic features (discourse, vocabulary, and syntax) to maintain or subvert power.

Had Ms. Albertson viewed language as solely vocabulary, she likely would not have highlighted the essential language structures in the target math problem or emphasized how specific language choices and features reflected disciplinary ways of thinking about multiple method solutions or the manipulation of different mathematical representations. Furthermore, the contributions of students, including Arav, Jamie, Juanita, Remy, and Julia, would not have been viewed as facilitative for promoting language learning, but instead as potentially impeding language learning. Instead, the student contributions and voices throughout this chapter are instructive in their use of language and demonstrate the linguistic fluidity that is essential for equitable language teaching. For educators, understanding student contributions as assets for language teaching and learning is only possible with a more multifaceted understanding of language. This means evaluating not only the words and terms used, but also attending to how language is taken up for communicating different purposes in critical and intentional ways to empower student contributions and voice. Language-awareness inquiry routines are intended to elicit these rich student contributions so teachers and students can work together to critique and analyze the power and role of language in learning and, ultimately, transform students' sense of belonging in the classroom.

CHAPTER 4 CLOSING REFLECTION

Now that you have read some classroom examples and learned more about how vocabulary fits into larger language structures that support an author's message, how would you revise your responses to the Chapter 4 Reflection? To apply your developing knowledge of language-awareness inquiry routines, what transformational and metalinguistic prompts might guide a lesson you are currently working on? What disciplinary scripts would you highlight and what discourse, syntax, and vocabulary do you want to address in your prompts?

Promoting a Path, Not a Phase

> **CONCEPTIONS THAT PROMOTE EQUITABLE LANGUAGE TEACHING**
>
> Language awareness that builds language fluidity is relevant for every age and stage.

Ms. Marshall (a White 1st-grade teacher), Ms. Angel (a Latina 3rd-grade science teacher), and Mr. Mitchell (a Southeast Asian 7th-grade science teacher) were sitting together in the teachers' lounge of their K–8, urban, Midwestern school. Ms. Marshall recounted a story about a beloved 1st-grader who was really puzzled by the phrase "falling in love" and how this language inspired lots of intentional falling to the ground each time he talked about loving something or someone. She explained that his exuberance for meatballs resulted in a staged fall gone awry and a visit to the nurse's office. Ms. Marshall laughed, saying, "Loving meatballs should not be so painful!" Mr. Mitchell responded by describing a recent lesson in his science class when he also attempted to make abstract language more concrete and tangible. To help students understand the porousness of a cell, he set up an elaborate simulation that included spaghetti noodles. He bemoaned the unclean state of his classroom at the end of the period and the noodles jammed in his desk drawer. He joked about the pasta in his desk: "The cell wall is flexible, but it is also sturdy and NOT that mobile." Ms. Marshall turned to her colleagues and said, "The kinds of conversations we have about language at each grade are hilarious and messy in different ways." Ms. Angel nodded and smiled. Later, Ms. Angel elaborated that she and Mr. Mitchell often talk about the role language plays in their classrooms and, while the language and content-specific terms they use vary, the language teaching they engage in with their students also feels "deeply and totally related."

CHAPTER 5 REFLECTION

Take a moment to think about how you see the language demands of learning in elementary, middle, and high school. Do you agree with Ms. Angel? Why or why not? Mr. Mitchell is currently teaching a unit on how living things respond to and change in their environment, and Ms. Angel is teaching a unit on animal species and their characteristics. Based on your response to Ms. Angel's comment, where do you see potential areas of overlap or difference in language teaching for these two science teachers?

Ms. Marshall is not alone in seeing language teaching and learning in kindergarten through 12th grade as different. Many of the educators we have worked with question whether, given the distinctive demands of disciplinary learning and specialized texts in the upper grades, we can think about language in the same way across elementary, middle, and secondary school. Ms. Marshall's view that language should be conceptualized and approached differently in the upper and lower grades is instantiated by educational resources that focus primarily on just one stage of schooling (Shanahan & Shanahan, 2008; Buehl, 2011; Gottlieb & Ernst-Slavit, 2014; Zwiers, 2013; Zwiers & Hamerla, 2018). Instead, we argue that language-awareness inquiry routines can connect the practices and strategies that support equitable language teaching in the early grades with those emphasized in middle and high school settings. We explicitly link practices for multiple age groups to provide a resource for teachers across the grade span. Although we recognize that sometimes language demands do vary, we provide a set of tools to expose these demands and differences and create a wealth of opportunities for students' varied linguistic resources over the course of their entire development.

SCHOOL TEXT: CHALLENGE AND OPPORTUNITY

To tackle differences and continuity in language teaching for a range of ages, we begin with a discussion of school texts and the distinctive demands of these texts across the grade span. Our focus on school texts (e.g., textbooks, photocopied handouts, novels) does not reflect a stance that these resources and materials *should* be the gold standard. On the contrary, many of the texts used by schools maintain and reify existing oppressive structures in their overrepresentation of White authors, specific ways of knowing, and language structures that do not represent the youth in our classrooms. Instead, we start with an exploration of the language demands of school texts because they are often prescribed by schools and districts and thus present a challenge and an opportunity for teachers eager to enact teaching of these texts in ways that bolster students' linguistic fluidity and validate students' unique language assets. While some scholars recommend removing these texts entirely in favor of texts that more directly reflect students' lived experiences, particularly of Black students (Baker-Bell, 2020b), we recognize that this is not always possible for many teachers who are beholden to certain curricular materials tied to state standards. Additionally, adopting texts intended to highlight the lived experiences of students in linguistically diverse classrooms or multiethnic classrooms can sometimes have the unintended consequence of performatively celebrating student differences or tokenizing students.

An approach to teaching language that equips students and teachers with tools to combat racism and discrimination (Lee, 2007) can lead to deeper conversations about power, privilege, and language. Language awareness inquiry routines offer teachers a framework for asking questions that draw attention to language features that are distinctive and less familiar to students, especially with texts that are traditionally more marginalizing to linguistic and ethnic minoritized groups. We provide strategies for teachers working with the demands of state standards—demands that change over time—and support teachers in asking questions that unpack language in school texts that can be marginalizing or foreign, while simultaneously encouraging teachers to frame these questions alongside larger discussions about language, power, and transformation.

Different Demands of School Texts Across Grades

Language-awareness inquiry routines can provide a consistent framework for how to approach teaching across grades despite shifts in the language demands of school texts and standards at different grade levels. Over time, as students' content learning becomes more specialized, school texts become denser and more precise in their discipline-specific language. Content area classes require a subject-specific knowledge set, which increases the demand for information presented with concise and dense language structures (Nagy & Townsend, 2012). For example, a 2nd-grade, elementary-level text on snakes might read:

> Snakes come in all shapes and sizes. Even though they do not have limbs, these reptiles can slither, climb, swim, burrow and glide. Snakes can be found on every continent except Antarctica and some species even live in the ocean. (Starkey, 2020)

Whereas a 7th-grade, middle school–level text on the same subject will look more like:

> A snake that lives in tall, green grass may *benefit* from being green. In this environment, a green snake will be able to hide from predators more easily than a brown snake will. Therefore, green snakes will *survive and reproduce* more than brown snakes will. But being brown may be more beneficial if the snake lives on a forest floor that has a large amount of dead leaves. On a forest floor, a brown snake will probably survive and reproduce more than a green snake will. (Holt California Life Science, 2007)

To elaborate on these distinctive language demands across grade levels, it's important to highlight critical language structures and features. Key features of language teaching in content area classrooms include the disciplinary script (i.e., how to perform traditional thinking, being, and knowledge sharing in history, math, or science), discourse (how the text is organized and structured), vocabulary (what the words mean) and syntax (how the ideas are linked) of a text. The discourse of the elementary 2nd-grade science text is focused on informing the reader about characteristics of snakes (i.e., the structure focuses on defining a concept). The vocabulary (e.g., burrow, continent, and species) and syntax (e.g., "Even though") are challenging for a 2nd-grader, but the conceptual understanding is relatively concrete and straightforward. That is, this text answers: What does this animal look like, move like, and where does it live? In the middle-school text, the ideas are more abstract and the language is more dense and specialized, necessitating certain ways of connecting ideas and more challenging discourse structures associated with science meaning-making. Unlike the elementary text in which each sentence begins with "snakes" or "they," the middle school text varies in the subject of the sentence "In this environment" or "But being brown may be more beneficial" and does so to draw the reader's attention to the disciplinary knowledge that environmental factors influence the experience of living beings, with certain animal traits or characteristics serving animals in only certain environments and being necessary for survival. These ideas are at the core of scientific (disciplinary) scripts or approaches about cause-and-effect relationships in the real world and principles of change and adaptation (see Figure 5.1 for a list of key features for language teaching in each text).

Language-awareness inquiry routines; processes of question asking that draws students' attention to these language features; and the relationship between language, power, and belonging can be used across grade levels and content areas to illuminate these aspects of texts. In this case, language-awareness inquiry routines can be used to highlight sensemaking

Figure 5.1. Elementary and Middle School Texts on Snakes' Key Features

Core Language Features	2nd-Grade Snake Text	7th-Grade Snake Text
Disciplinary Script	Meaning-making in life science	Meaning-making in evolutionary biology
Discourse/Text Frame	Concept/definition text frame	Cause/effect text frame
Vocabulary	Burrow, continent, species	Survive, reproduce, benefit, predators
Syntax	Connectives: "Even though," "even," "except"	Varied subject: "In this environment" "on a forest floor" "But being brown"

about the scientific world and the language associated with science scripts. Teachers can use a similar framework to develop language-awareness inquiry prompts that target language features particular to their specific grade level and respective class.

Both reptile texts grapple with how snakes' physical characteristics relate to how they live (see Figure 5.2 for metalinguistic prompts—questions that help students reflect on and manipulate these language features—at each of these grade levels).

In the elementary text, students learn that a limbless creature can live in the ocean and swim or can burrow and climb if they live in the mountains, surviving in varied circumstances even without arms or legs. To access this information using the metalinguistic question "What do snakes look like and do, what scientific language provides clues to help you figure this out?", students must attend to language in the text that tells them about how something is and how it changes. In the middle school text, students can access the text by asking similar questions about what the text is communicating using particular language, i.e., "How and why do snakes change form? What scientific language provides clues for why they change form?" Answers to these questions across grades exist on a related continuum of observation about salient animal characteristics and how these characteristics change and are influenced by their environment. It is the level of conceptual complexity that varies across texts and the language that describes and evokes snakes that shifts in concert. Said another way, teaching students to approach these texts with attention to language features about observing living things (e.g., words that signal their color, shape, and size) and language choices for connecting ideas about how beings function in the world (e.g., language that signals cause and effect relationships with "therefore" or exceptional cases with the use of "except") should be constant regardless of grade level. And, while this constant attention to language structures and markers will remain consistent across time, the difficulty of the content and by extension the level of abstraction of the language in the text will require more fine-grained attention to these language features in higher grades than lower grades.

Language choices at the word, sentence, and discourse level leveraged for disciplinary script purposes can and should be addressed across grades.

Figure 5.2. Language-Awareness Inquiry Routine Prompts for Metalinguistic Aims

	2nd Grade	7th Grade
Metalinguistic Language-Awareness Inquiry Prompts	What do snakes look like and do? What scientific language provides clues to help you figure this out?	How and why do snakes change form? What scientific language provides clues for why they change form?

However, the specificity with which they are addressed will vary by grade level, as texts in the older grades include:

1. More precise, specialized discipline-specific words (Nagy & Townsend, 2012),
2. Denser presentation of information (Bailey, 2007; Nagy & Townsend, 2012),
3. More linguistic markers of conceptual relationships (if, then or first, second, and lastly) (Bailey, 2007; Schleppegrell, 2004; Uccelli et al., 2013), and
4. More language that expresses abstract ideas (Nagy & Townsend, 2012: Schleppegrell, 2004; Snow & Uccelli, 2009).

Figure 5.3 compares these four characteristics of texts using our two snake passages. We highlight these characteristics to emphasize that adolescence is a period of time where students are encountering texts with language choices that serve more specialized disciplinary purposes, providing an opportunity for a more robust and critical understanding of these characteristics of texts (Blum-Kulka, 2008; Berman & Ravid, 2009).

These shifts in text language characteristics across grade levels is even more evident when we compare them with high school texts. A high school biology textbook might read:

> Other animals have evolved different structures to give them support and protection. Invertebrates, such as sea urchins and sea stars, have an internal skeleton called an endoskeleton, which is covered by layers of cells. It provides support for an animal's body. The endoskeleton protects internal organs and provides an internal brace for muscles to pull against. (Glencoe Biology, 2002)

This paragraph, focused on describing the role and function of the endoskeleton for invertebrates, includes a wealth of specialized scientific vocabulary (e.g., "invertebrates," "endoskeleton," "cells," "organs," "urchins") and dense information. For example, the second sentence includes both embedded examples as well as informative descriptions. Explicit markers of relationships between ideas and concepts are evident such as language like "other animals," used to draw a comparison between invertebrates and vertebrates. Lastly, the ideas in this high school paragraph and the language to capture these ideas is abstract. For example, the idea of an internal protection structure that is not visible is described with an analogy about the endoskeleton being equivalent to an internal brace for muscles to pull against.

As illustrated in Figure 5.3, these same language characteristics are present in the middle school snake text, with this text including precise science vocabulary (e.g., survive, reproduce, beneficial, reproduce), a density

Figure 5.3. Characteristics of Text Language Across Passages

Language Characteristics of Text That Increase Over the Course of Schooling	2nd-Grade Text	7th-Grade Text	Greater Language Demands of Adolescent Texts
Precise and specialized vocabulary	"Shapes and sizes"	"Survive and reproduce"	The 7th-grade text is using specialized terms essential to meaning-making in science to describe complex processes compared with the less precise language used to describe snake characteristics in the 3rd-grade text.
Information density	"Snakes come in all shapes and sizes."	"In this environment, a green snake will be able to hide from predators more easily than a brown snake will."	The 7th-grade text includes a wealth of ideas in one sentence and does so by using language that specifies the beneficial environment for a green snake and that highlights the comparison between a green snake and a brown snake.
Markers of relationships between concepts and ideas	"Even though," "except"	"Therefore," "but," "more easily," "more than"	The 7th-grade text uses many more explicit discourse markers to clarify causal relationships, with words like "therefore" and relationships of comparison such as "more easily" or "more than."
Abstract ideas	"Snakes are ambulatory even without limbs."	Survival of the fittest	The 7th-grade text captures an idea that is more abstract in that it requires students to understand not just the here and now but the idea of generations.

of information (e.g., "But being brown may be more beneficial if the snake lives on a forest floor that has a large amount of dead leaves"), a fair number of linguistic markers of relationships between ideas (e.g., "more easily"), and a relatively high level of abstraction (e.g. the concept of adaptation and survival of the fittest). Comparing the language across these texts reveals a clear progression in linguistic precision, specialization, density, and abstractness. Viewing all three texts in combination, we can see that these language characteristics exist on a continuum, but across all texts, attention to language markers is useful.

Although language-awareness inquiry routine prompts across texts will be different, all of the prompts should focus on identifying language clues about characteristics of a living being and science scripts. If we return to Ms. Marshall and Mr. Mitchell and their teachers' lounge language discussion, the same is true. "Falling in love" and "porous cell membranes" both represent language that captures abstract ideas. Drawing attention to their abstraction is critical for teaching students about linguistic fluidity, and how language can be used to convey abstract ideas with language that is equally symbolic and metaphysical. The same linguistic features warrant attention and critique, but the precision, specialization, density, explicitness, and abstractness change as students progress in school.

Through the use of metalinguistic questions that explore language choices and demands at the discourse, sentence, and word level, language-awareness inquiry routines set students up for success. They help to support a habit of language exploration that encourages students to construct meaning from complex texts while also empowering more fluid use of language to understand how information is being presented. To help students identify these aspects of language and critique them across multiple texts, lessons, and disciplinary contexts, language awareness inquiry routine prompts also include transformative questions about how language can include or exclude and how to empower belonging through language choices and interrogation. Transformative and metalinguistic questions are applicable at each grade and for each content area, and they become more powerful as a tool when students can see this consistent focus across ages and spaces.

Across classrooms, teachers can use metalinguistic prompts about vocabulary, syntax, and discourse to ask questions about how the language of their content area texts are distinctive and identify how these language structures communicate meaning for a specific disciplinary purpose, context, and audience. Teachers can couple these questions with transformational prompts that focus on the intersection of language and power and disciplinary exclusion. These prompts should highlight how content is communicated in ways that privilege certain types of knowledge or ways of being and provide students with opportunities to think about the ways they do and don't want to take up certain linguistic forms in more conscious and critical ways.

Figure 5.4. Transformational Language-Awareness Inquiry Prompts Across Grades

Grade	2nd-Grade Science Text	7th-Grade Science Text	High School Biology Text
Transformational Prompt	Are there other ways to talk about what we observe? If we think about the five senses, what is included and what is left out in science? Does this leave out an important part of our experience that we wish to express?	Science focuses through language choices on processes and evidence. Does this focus exclude some knowledge over others? What evidence from the world is valued?	Is some language scientific and some language is not? How is scientific language used to wield power and influence?

In Figure 5.4 we provide some sample transformational prompts across the grades that are intended to cut across several lessons. These examples are content specific, attending to science's preoccupation with observing the natural world in particular ways and attention to ordered processes for the 2nd-grade and 7th-grade texts, respectively. Across grades the precision, specialization, density, explicitness, and abstractness of language changes. Equitable language instruction requires a consistent exploration of language features, linguistic fluidity, and student empowerment no matter the grade level.

CLASSROOM LANGUAGE CONVERSATIONS ACROSS THE GRADES

Classroom texts can serve as a springboard for rich conversations about language structures and the relationship between language and power through language-awareness inquiry routines. These conversations are fruitful spaces for building linguistic fluidity as students develop a wealth of knowledge about disciplinary scripts and their particular language features. In our observations of classrooms across the country, discussions in elementary and secondary classrooms sounded different in many of the same ways that grade-level texts differ. In the beginning of this chapter, Ms. Marshall raises the issue that discussions about language are distinctive in elementary, middle, and high school settings. We argue that language-awareness inquiry routines forge a consistent path to linguistic awareness and by extension student success across grades. Classroom conversations help to achieve this goal by constantly highlighting language unique to specific texts, classrooms, and grades. Encouraging and supporting students in using this same framework and analytic lens across grade levels to interrogate what they hear, read, write, and say supports the development of linguistically fluid schools that welcome all students' language resources. To illustrate cross-grade continuity and the simultaneous flexibility to tailor the conversation to distinctive language demands in each grade, we describe two classrooms—one kindergarten and the other from middle school.

A Discussion in a Kindergarten Classroom

We visited Ms. May's kindergarten classroom on several occasions over the course of the year. Ms. May, a White monolingual teacher, works in an urban school in the Northeast. Her class is culturally and linguistically diverse, with many students coming from different countries and living in homes where a language other than English is spoken. In October, Ms. May's class was talking about the difference between asking questions and making statements. This language distinction at first glance does not seem discipline-specific, yet understanding the difference between inquiry and stance is an essential building block for disciplinary meaning-making around mathematical problem-solving or the art of persuasion in the later grades.

Ms. May sees this lesson as critical for crafting a learning community where students can gain knowledge from their peers and acquire additional tools for self-expression. To support students in understanding the difference between questions and comments, Ms. May attends to language features that signal these distinct purposes. She begins the lesson by posing the question, "What language helps us ask questions and what language helps us tell something we know?" This initial question is aligned with her metalinguistic aim and scaffolds subsequent language-awareness inquiry routine prompts around how language markers signal purpose. She will follow this prompt with more fine-grained questions that support dissecting the language of inquiry and stance at the discourse, syntax, and vocabulary levels. She explains that they will discuss these different ways of talking about sharing information and expressing how one feels or what they know.

Ms. May's learning activity involves telling students about an experience she had. She explains to the students that she went to see a detective because she could not find her favorite red shoe. She reminds the class that detectives ask questions to figure out and solve mysteries and that she wants to know if they think the detective asked useful questions and why or why not. She draws students' attention to the board where she has the sentence frame "I wonder __________?" with the words "why," "how," "what," "when," "who," and "where" floating above this sentence frame on the board. The week before this lesson, Ms. May helped students come up with questions for each of the six different question types to identify an object they were touching while blindfolded. She showed how these question stems could help them figure out what the hidden object was. Her attention to the question stems supports students in attending to language that helps them understand a speaker's purpose.

Ms. May shares the first question the detective asked her: "Where was the last place you saw your shoe?" She smiles and looks at Marco and uses a set of questions that support the kind of language-awareness inquiry she hopes to instill in her students: "Is that a question? And, why or why not?" He nods. She follows up with, "How do you know? What language helps you figure it out?" He points to the question stems on the board and says, "You said 'where'!" Ms. May follows up with, "Yes, I used 'where' and why might this help me find my shoe?" Marco thinks for eight seconds and then responds, "Maybe it is still there?" She enthusiastically responds to his insight, "Yes! It is a good question because he asked me 'where,' and the answer might tell us where it still is or if it moved!" She turns to the class and says, "And then the detective said, 'When did you last see your shoes?'" She then asks the students to turn to each other and decide if this was a question and why or why not and what language helped them figure it out. She listens attentively to the different pairs, circling the room and asking each pair again, "Why is it a question?" pushing them to provide responses that include both the question stem and an understanding of whether the potential response provided by Ms. May might help uncover an additional clue for the missing shoe.

After a couple of additional examples, she says, "And then the detective said, 'Oh your shoes are red. I love red.'" She pauses and looks at the students. Again, she encourages the children to turn and talk and consider whether this is a question and why or why not. She circles the room, listening to students talking with each other. Then she writes their ideas on the board: "It doesn't have a question word in it." "The detective is telling something." "Ms. May doesn't have to say any words or anything." She creates a chart with a question mark on the left side and a mouth on the right, writing all the question types under the question mark and writing student ideas about the language of comments or personal contributions on the other side (e.g., "comments begin with I love, I think, I feel" etc.). She reads these ideas aloud from the anchor chart to her students. She synthesizes their observations and explains that the detective was making a statement or comment that tells about something but does not ask anything.

Then Ms. May asks students to turn to each other and talk about a question they might have about her shoe. She writes these under the question side of the chart and in a box at the top she writes the things the students know so far about her shoe's disappearance. Then, she has them turn to each other and come up with a comment they might make. As children talk about their comments and questions, Ms. May has them explain how they know whether something is a comment or a question. She also asks a couple of students to pretend to be the detective and ask questions and comments, with students using a thumbs up or thumbs down to determine whether a question posed is a good one.

She circulates the room listening to their conversations. Yohan and Mirabel are laughing together as Ms. May approaches them on the rug. Mirabel recently emigrated from Columbia and Yohan was born in the United States, but his parents were born in Jamaica. Mirabel is still more comfortable speaking Spanish and her English vocabulary is still developing. Yohan explains that Mirabel asks the best questions, and he starts saying to Mirabel "Show her, show her." Mirabel smiles and says, "Where shoe?" she holds her palms up to the ceiling moving them fast and opens her eyes wide with her mouth a little open. Her curiosity and interest physically manifest in the eagerness of her hands bouncing up and down awaiting an answer. Yohan shows that he asked Mirabel a question really clearly by raising his eyebrow (he proudly explains that his dad taught him how to move his eyebrows to communicate) while using a question word. Ms. May was excited about their conversation and in the way they highlighted gesture, as yet another way we can communicate our intentions. Ms. May brings this idea back to the class, with Mirabel and Yohan using their distinguishing gestures. Consistent with existing research (Holler et al., 2018), the class agrees that these gestures communicate quickly and efficiently that the speaker is asking a question. Ms. May adds to her anchor chart different gestures that might accompany these different ways of communicating and discusses how the gestures themselves communicate eagerness or confusion, in the case of questions. The class starts brainstorming ways they and their families use gestures to communicate thoughts and ideas.

At the end of the lesson, the location of the shoe is revealed, students understand more about how to request information as well as how to share something they know, feel, or think, and how to compare and contrast two types of talk (inquiry requests and personal contributions). This lesson did not include knowledge of what we might think of as disciplinary or subject area content, but it does provide essential building blocks for language discussions in the later grades about more abstract concepts. Students are engaging in important language work here. They are learning to compare and contrast how two ways of talk are different (three, if you include gesture!) and how language reveals these differences. They are engaging in patterns of thinking that attend to how language signals getting information (i.e., asking questions that help them gain relevant details). They are articulating personal ideas and perspectives (i.e., I think, I feel, I know, and I do). And, they are learning how the language markers that accompany these different intentions can serve as guideposts for understanding a speaker's goals or for articulating their own.

This particular lesson is more teacher directed than many of Ms. May's lessons. She used it as an anchor lesson about linguistic markers that support two different types of intentions (i.e., getting information versus sharing a personal perspective) that served as the bedrock for lessons that followed, such as a lesson where students played different roles learning about different seasons, with members of each group designated as the questioner (determining good questions to ask about characteristics of seasons) and the persuader (convincing others of their opinion of the best season). Throughout both lessons, students developed their linguistic fluidity across types of talk (inquiry or stance) and forms of communication (talking and gesture). Specifically, they were able to recognize how language is used in different ways, and the value of their own linguistic insights. These lessons revealed that they can use what they already know (e.g., raised eyebrows to communicate a question) to support their learning.

Planning for Action for the Classroom

Early Grade Tips

1. Generate prompts that focus attention on language related to exclusion/inclusion, ways of participating, and student contributions (transformative).
2. Generate prompts that help students reflect on how particular language supports specific purposes and goals (metalinguistic).
3. Draw attention to language structures and organization.
4. Highlight, define, use, and question vocabulary for learning and talking about content.
5. Provide sentence frames that support talking about content, and equally important, promote reflection and questioning around how ideas are linked in a particular way for meaning-making.

Ms. May supported her students with overarching transformational prompts (i.e., "How does language help us get what we want and need? How can everyone participate?") that framed several lessons, and homed in on the topic of questions versus comments with targeted metalinguistic questions (i.e., "What language helps us ask questions? How does it do that?"). Her lesson focused students' attention on the language structures or discourse of comparing/contrasting with her prompts asking them to distinguish between questions (inquiry) and comments (stance) in her story. She provided friendly definitions and multiple exposures through her own modeling and peer sharing of the words: exploring, detecting, describing, and commenting, among other words. Lastly, she prompted students to use sentence frames like "I wonder. . . why, what, where, how. . . ." to answer her questions about the missing shoe and to think about how gestures, question words (e.g., "what," "where," "how"), and transition words (e.g., "but") signal the speaker's intention.

A Discussion in a Middle School Classroom

Mr. Mercedes, a White bilingual (Spanish and English) social studies teacher, works in an urban, largely Black neighborhood in the Midwest. When we observed his 7th-grade class, his students had just read a text about the science behind vaccines and the beliefs of anti-vaxxers. The article the class read contained sentences such as, "For many countries, certain immunizations are obligatory for school entry. In the United States, state laws require vaccinations for students to enter school. However, for many the issue of vaccination is complicated and is influenced by social and historical factors." The article included multiple perspectives on vaccination and focused on issues related to individual freedoms and the public good. The text largely followed a proposition/support text frame in that it presented a viewpoint that was then argued and supported. As Mr. Mercedes reviewed this text with his students, he used several metalinguistic probes to support their understanding of the discourse, syntax, and vocabulary in the article.

After dissecting the article, Mr. Mercedes showed students some data that included a simulation of the speed at which a virus can spread. He asked students to indicate by walking to a designated quadrant of the room whether they thought: Schools, without exception, should have the right to require students be vaccinated (position 1); schools should have the right, with exception of extreme circumstances (position 2); schools should not have the right most of the time (position 3); or schools should not have the right under any circumstances (position 4). Based on student answers, Mr. Mercedes put students in heterogeneous groups with students holding varied positions. The groups were tasked with coming to a consensus about a sole position that they would need to advocate for to the whole class.

When reading the text with students, Mr. Mercedes highlighted certain language associated with articulating a perspective, and engaged in language-awareness inquiry routines that drew students' attention to language features related to how the author provided evidence for their perspective. In the activity in which students had to defend their own positions, Mr. Mercedes had students think about sentence frames/starters that would help them persuade their peers with a clear argument and substantive evidence. The class came up with the following sentence starters that asked students to:

- Elaborate
    - » Can you say more about __________?
- Clarify
    - » I am not sure I understand your point. Can you clarify __________?
- Disagree
    - » He/She/They argue __________, however I argue __________.

- Agree
    - I agree because _________.
    - I agree and also think _________.
- Provide detail or evidence
    - Evidence to support _________ is _________.
    - Another example is _________.
    - On page _________ the text says _________.
    - In my experience, _________.
    - It is common knowledge that _________.
- Take a stand
    - We should not _________ because _________.

Mr. Mercedes has also talked with the students about some of the vocabulary in the passage, including what was meant by "individual rights," the "public good," and "immunity." He also highlighted words critical to the debate that were less discipline-specific—some from the text and some he believed were relevant for talking about the text—that he thought would help them discuss these core terms, such as "outweigh," "privilege," and "risk." As students discussed and debated the arguments for and against making vaccinations obligatory in schools, they were explicitly encouraged to use evidence from the text they read, the data they reviewed, or from personal experience, and to draw from the sentence starters on the board. Mr. Mercedes circled the room, listening to students' conversations and asking them to provide evidence for their arguments. He took notes on their comments for the purpose of synthesizing some of their persuasive talk moves at the end of their group conversations.

Once Mr. Mercedes noticed that most groups had come to some level of consensus, he asked the groups to present to the whole class their position and their process. That is, he asked what persuaded those who changed their minds and why those arguments were compelling, particularly the language used. Focusing specifically on the process, students described a personal anecdote about a peer's sibling whose university shut down because of a cluster of measles cases and disrupted learning for everyone was particularly compelling. Other students explained how one student's argument about the simulation data and how fast a disease could spread encouraged more of a focus on the importance of public good over individual freedom. Multiple students highlighted particular group members as being especially persuasive in how they were able to contradict other students by providing counter examples (e.g., "Well, but you can't bring guns to school. Are you saying we should be free to bring guns?") or pressed peers for evidence (e.g., "But the article said it [the vaccine] didn't mess anybody up, so fear is just not . . . not persuasive. I don't believe it. Give me an example to believe it.") in ways that revealed a flaw in a peer's argument.

Mr. Mercedes wrote on the board the types of evidence students found compelling (i.e., personal examples, data examples, and examples from the article) and the kinds of student talk that was particularly persuasive (i.e., "counterarguments," "requests for evidence," and "student tone or stance"). Mr. Mercedes synthesized students' remarks, commenting on how persuasive students were when they used counterarguments to defend their position and how students provided more detail or asked for more detail in ways that served to persuade or undermine others. When asked to think specifically about the language their peers had used that was particularly persuasive, many students highlighted language that was passionate such as "it is clear" and "I feel confident that"; language that included a double negative like "never, not once"; or language that was very detailed, for example, "On page 5 of the article it says. . . ."

Mr. Mercedes's lesson honed students' ability to debate and discuss ideas in social studies, and their skill at understanding how language choices matter for persuasion. He also built on the students' language to highlight how oral disciplinary scripts provide unique opportunities for analysis (e.g., the repetition of the word "not" to negate something fervently). At the end of the lesson, students were asked in their groups to write a list of reasons to support their position, which would be given to one of the groups that had a different position. Mr. Mercedes encouraged them to draw from the student-generated list of language on the board that was particularly persuasive, such as using rich details (e.g., the speed of spread from the data, a juicy quote from the article), examples of evidence (e.g., no fatal side effects), and language that signals a strong stance (e.g., "without a doubt . . ." or "You ain't never seen . . .").

Planning for Action for the Classroom

Upper Grade Tips

1. Generate prompts that focus attention on how language can instantiate power and difference and ways to empower student voice (transformative).
2. Generate prompts that help students reflect on language, and use metalanguage (i.e., language about language) to discuss language use for specific purposes (metalinguistic).
3. Draw attention to language structures and markers of conceptual relationships.
4. Highlight, define, use, and question vocabulary that is specialized, supports talk about the content, and expresses abstract ideas.
5. Provide sentence frames to support talking about content and, equally important, promote reflection and critique around how

ideas are linked in ways that can pack information and promote certain types of meaning-making.

In this lesson, Mr. Mercedes drew from a larger overarching transformative prompt that has guided several of his lessons this week on how certain language exerts power, why, and whether it should have that power (i.e., "Does certain language persuade when it comes to debate? Why? Should it?"). He coupled these prompts with metalinguistic questions (i.e., "What language helps us persuade and make an argument? What language provides evidence?") that helped students explore a more circumscribed critique of the language of the focal text. His lesson focused their attention on the language structures or discourse of proposition/support by having them dissect the different positions in the article and build their own argument from the text. He provided explicit and accessible definitions and multiple exposures through the texts, his own modeling, and peer interactions to the words: vaccination, individual rights, public good, outweigh, privilege, argument, and persuade, among other words. He prompted student to use sentence frames like "Evidence to support . . . is" or "He argues . . . however, I argue . . . " to address his request that they defend a position and provide evidence and troubled whether other ways of talking (e.g., double negatives) can be persuasive too and why.

Mr. Mercedes's debate and Ms. May's discussion have different language demands, but students across grade levels were all able to generate and engage in a rich linguistic space attentive to the unique language features of the content being discussed. Both teachers also showcased student language that provided students with opportunities to fluidly move between different language structures and conventions. Mr. Mercedes's class discussion included more specialized vocabulary, complex connectives, explicit markers in the sentence frames, and more abstract ideas and principles than Ms. May's discussion. However, as shown in Figure 5.5, both teachers focused students' attention on how language features help convey specific information for a particular purpose. They did this by using language-awareness inquiry routines as a guide for their lesson with preplanned metalinguistic prompts and an overarching transformative prompt to guide several lessons on these language structures and conventions. Additionally, both teachers thoughtfully integrated students' contributions that drew attention to the way language was being used by students for a particular purpose.

Students' unique contributions and language expertise are at the core of teachers' transformative inquiry prompts in each example. In both

Figure 5.5. Linguistic Features of Ms. May's and Mr. Mercedes's Class Discussions

Language Feature	Kindergarten	7th Grade	Common Ground
Disciplinary Script	How does language help us get what we want and need? How can everyone participate? (transformative) What language helps us ask questions? How does it do that? (metalinguistic) What language helps us tell about something we know? How does it do that? (metalinguistic)	Does certain language persuade when it comes to debate? Why? Should it? (transformative) What language helps us persuade and make an argument? (metalinguistic) What language provides evidence? (metalinguistic)	Discussed the role language plays in the targeted purpose at the beginning, middle, and end of the lesson.
Discourse/ text-frame	Compare/Contrast	Proposition/ Support	The discourse is set as the purpose of the language features in the conversation/discussion and supports the synthesis at the end.
Syntax	"I wonder ______ why, what, where___." versus "I think, I feel, I know, and I do _____." "But _________."	"He argues ____ however, I argue _______." "Evidence to support ______ is. . . ." "Furthermore, we should not _______ because. . . ."	Students are provided with a wealth of language choices and resources to support meaning-making, which they evaluate as part of the discussion.
Vocabulary	Investigation, exploring, detecting, describing, commenting	Vaccination, individual rights, public good, outweigh, privilege	Some pre-teaching of vocabulary is used for new concepts, and students are encouraged to use language that helps them share their purpose with others.

classrooms, teachers used students' knowledge of language to support discussions about what kinds of language matter and language's place in supporting meaning-making. Both teachers saw student contributions (e.g., use of gestures and double negatives) as assets for pushing linguistic discussions to be more meta about the role of language in message crafting and delivery. This stance is a stark contrast to classrooms in which authentic student voices are seen as intrusions to the core lesson. Mr. Mercedes and Ms. May promote language awareness and by extension, linguistic fluidity and power. Both classrooms showcase the ways in which language differs across grades with regard to content (e.g., level of abstraction, density of words, discipline-specific concepts) and most frequent mode of instruction (discussion verses reading). But beyond these differences, a meaningful similarity cuts across grades. Both lessons aim to draw students' attention to how language reveals intentions and influences the message expressed.

CONCEPTUALIZING LANGUAGE AWARENESS ACROSS GRADES

Students are never too young or too old to consider the functional role of language for meaning-making and the power of language choices. Language teaching across all ages should focus on language-awareness inquiry routines that reveal how language supports or undermines different communicative purposes and the ways in which power is embedded in language use. A common misconception of language teaching is that primary grade language learning is fundamentally less rigorous. This misconception might lead one to deduce that the high school text on the endoskeleton or Mr. Mercedes's discussion on vaccinations are more "sophisticated" linguistically or that we should reserve such a fine-grained approach to language until the later grades. Instead, we encourage educators to reframe language teaching as about ways of using language to support the dissection of information presented in talk or text. This view of language teaching should neither create a hierarchy of sophistication, nor privilege certain ways of talking, reading, or writing. Teachers can create a pathway for language and content learning where students continuously build language-awareness skills. They can work with students across the grade span to analyze, manipulate, and reimagine language use to fulfill their own goals. Language-awareness inquiry routines support students in being able to investigate and interrogate the purposes of others, authors, and themselves, so they can gain knowledge and empower their own informed opinions, responses, and decisions. The nature of the language used varies but the attention to language is consistent, with the meticulousness with which language is critiqued and evaluated being no more or no less as a function of grade.

CHAPTER 5 CLOSING REFLECTION

Now that we have reviewed ways in which equitable language teaching is distinct and similar across the grades, take a moment to revisit your reflection responses at the start of this chapter. Analyze the assumptions and knowledge that helped you form your initial impressions. Ask yourself the following questions:

1. *What did you initially view as essential for language learning in the early grades and how did this inform your response?*
2. *How would your answers change now?*
3. *Can you think of a current lesson you teach or plan to teach and how that lesson might build on students' language awareness from a previous grade?*

Part III

COLLECTIVE INQUIRY: FORGING COMMUNITIES FOR EQUITY

CHAPTER 6

Taking a Collaborative Approach: Supporting Equitable Language Teaching Through Teams

> **Conceptions That Promote Equitable Language Teaching**
>
> For equitable language instruction, teachers need collaborative spaces to develop their professional sensemaking around linguistic fluidity.

Mr. Lesley (6th grade), Ms. Una (7th grade), and Ms. Elmer (8th grade)—three English language arts (ELA) educators teaching at the same middle school in the Northeast—are meeting to discuss lesson planning for their respective units focused on the texts *Number the Stars* (Lowry, 1989), *Roll of Thunder, Hear My Cry* (Taylor, 1976), and *Of Mice and Men* (Steinbeck, 1937). Recently they attended a workshop on posing questions that prompt students to engage with text segments and they are trying to implement these practices in their classrooms, while maintaining their focus on promoting equitable language teaching throughout the curriculum and school. In this particular meeting, Ms. Una is "pumped" because she has created a graphic organizer to accompany the short segments of text she has selected for careful study as part of the unit. She is hopeful that this chart will help her 7th-grade students keep track of the various characters in the target chapter and capture their personality traits as part of annotating the text for deeper meaning.

These dedicated teachers meet weekly during one of their planning periods to take turns giving each other feedback on their lesson plans, sometimes using schoolwide planning protocols to guide them. Their relationships, established over time and through a common focus on English language arts teaching, form a foundation for sharing feedback that is equal parts informative and encouraging. In this session, Ms. Elmer provides some critical feedback to Ms. Una: "I like the chart you created and I see how this will serve as a way to direct students' annotations of the text, but I don't think the graphic organizer helps students dig deep into the passage because it isn't drawing attention to *how* the author is showing different characters' influence and power (i.e., key themes in the text) through language." For a moment, Ms. Una thinks about this critique of the graphic organizer. Then, through some back-and-forth exchanges, the group ultimately decides that the current graphic organizer doesn't attend to the text's language enough or to the ways in which language can be used by authors to show characters' power relations.

Ms. Elmer shares with Ms. Una a graphic organizer she plans to use to help students think about how ableism—discrimination against people with disabilities and, in the case of this text, the main character's intellectual disability—is reified in *Of Mice and Men* through the characters' dialogue. Together, they create a revised organizer that has a column where the students can fill in quotes from the text (the narrator's words or a quote from another character), a character's name in another column as well as their relationship to the main character, a word or sentence describing characteristics of the character, and an explanation about how the words in the selected quote show the characters' attempts to exert power and autonomy, reifying or disrupting taken-for-granted assumptions about (dis)ability in Ms. Elmer's class and understandings of racial justice and power in Ms. Una's class. The revised graphic organizer will ideally support Ms. Una's whole group and small group discussion about the different characters. Mr. Lesley then voices his own concerns; he feels Ms. Una's lesson is not providing enough opportunities for all students to "practice" language needed to meet state standards or to demonstrate their agency as language users. He has seen how text-based discussions can often be dominated by students with more developed language skills or exclude those students designated as special education learners. He urges Ms. Una to consider how competing understandings of justice and power present in the text can be explored by students and what this will mean for the discussion norms in her class as she supports their use of the graphic organizer.

This interaction isn't rare at the Irvington K–8 School. Across grades, teachers meet weekly for 50 to 60 minutes to work with other teachers to plan their subject area units and create consistency in their instructional approach and practices. These three teachers often talk about this group as their "ELA hotline" that allows them to support each other in maximizing the efficacy of their lessons, minimize the stress of trying new instructional practices alone, and share pedagogical ideas and struggles. Over time, and with the development of trust among members of the group, these weekly meetings have become a central place where teachers interrogate their own understandings of language and explore how some ways of thinking might inadvertently foster classroom practices that can serve to create inequitable environments for language teaching and learning.

CHAPTER 6 REFLECTION

When you collaborate with other educators, what are your discussions primarily focused on (e.g., content, specific students, performance, daily logistics)? Does language and equity play a role in these conversations?

How might equitable language teaching be integrated into these existing conversations?

COLLABORATING FOR EQUITABLE LANGUAGE TEACHING

Research routinely shows that for instructional changes to be effective, they can't occur in just one classroom with just one teacher, but must involve multiple school stakeholders (Hopkins et al., 2013; Darling-Hammond et al., 2009; Elmore, 1996; Hill, 2004). Equitable language teaching involves dismantling and questioning broader sociopolitical systems and ideologies that reify linguistic prejudice both within and beyond the classroom. This work is best undertaken by groups of educators working in community to engage in collective inquiry (McClain et al., 2021). Yet, it is rarely the case that teacher collaboration is intentionally designed to create such opportunities. To grow teacher collaborations that promote equitable language teaching, we encourage teacher teams to support each other in two critical, interrelated ways:

1. Develop and maintain equitable language beliefs and conceptions while dismantling misconceptions that limit equitable language teaching
2. Utilize the principles that undergird language-awareness inquiry routine practices to design and implement aligned inquiry work across classrooms

Growing and sustaining these beliefs and pedagogical principles must be a whole-school effort that is supported by administrators, involves ongoing iterative interrogation of individual understandings of language and courageous communication amongst teachers, and includes collaboration with families (Khalifa et al., 2016). We focus on teachers collectively interrogating and utilizing principled practice because, while we advocate for a community-wide effort, teachers remain central drivers of efficacious practice (Chetty et al., 2014), students' school engagement, and success (Gelhbach et al., 2012; Roorda et al., 2011). We explore the critical role and function of teacher teams by first addressing general principles and approaches for teamwork that can support equitable language teaching. We then discuss two features of teaming that are particularly critical to the practices described in this book to support equitable language teaching: adaptive teaching and collaborative professional sensemaking. We promote these two approaches to instruction because moving toward an equity-centered approach requires both reflection and action. Teachers can dig into and enact this work in teams to develop a united thinking, logic, and set of tools, and at the same time, center the unique demands and opportunities of individual classrooms.

HOW SUCCESSFUL TEACHER TEAMS PROMOTE EQUITY THROUGH LANGUAGE TEACHING

Teacher collaborations, and specifically teacher teamwork (teaming) or professional learning communities (PLCs) for instructional improvement or innovation, should be guided by the intentional use of structured routines, protocols, or cycles. In successful PLC groups, the focus is not only on so-called "visible behaviors of teaching" (Kennedy, 2016), but also on how teachers' thoughts, identities, knowledge, and actions come to be intertwined in enacted instruction. At their best, these groups examine how beliefs and understandings of language and language teaching animate the teaching of language in the classroom in ways that are equitable (Kennedy, 2016; Philip et al., 2019). Professional learning spaces that support equitable language teaching should offer educators opportunities to (Vedder-Weiss et al., 2018):

- Examine authentic, rich representations of equitable language teaching (whether through viewing videos of practice, reading case studies, studying the lessons of others, or probing lessons of their own design);
- Connect language teaching, language learning, and subject matter;
- Explore the instructional "problem" of implementing equitable language teaching by analyzing and seeking to understand it; and
- Position educators as capable of implementing these equitable language teaching practices in their own classrooms.

In practice, these aspects of high-efficacy professional learning are how teacher teams engage with the broader concept of equitable language teaching. The activities undertaken in teacher teams do much to shape the impact of professional learning. Having implemented these activities with in-service educators in our own work, we know firsthand how these practices offer an informal "curriculum" to effectively guide teacher teams in their sensemaking around equitable language teaching. However, the goal of these activities is not only to equip educators with new practices to teach language more equitably, but also to help them engage with the beliefs and commitments that bolster equitable language instruction. Consistent with existing research (Lynch, 2017; Hanno, 2022), we view teacher beliefs and instructional practices as bidirectional; that is, they influence each other, with teacher beliefs influencing teacher practice and teacher practice often influencing or changing beliefs (Enderle et al., 2014; Opfer & Pedder, 2011).

In Figure 6.1, we provide examples of structured frameworks for effective teamwork, including van Es and Sherin's (2008) video club, Lampert et al.'s (2013) rehearsals, or Bryk et al.'s (2015) (Plan-Do-Study-Act) or PDSA cycles for school improvement.

Figure 6.1. Structured Ways of Engaging in PLC Work

Authors	Type of Model	Description of Model for Improvement
van Es and Sherin (2008)	Framework	Provided a framework to support teacher noticing while watching teaching videos in community
Bryk and colleagues (2015)	Cycle	Provided a cycle for improving schools that includes a step-by-step process of being able to create action steps for meaningful purposes, engage in those steps and collect data, analyze the data, and decide how to act upon that data and then plan further steps
Lampert and colleagues (2013)	Simulations	Used detailed rehearsals or simulations of a learning event to support educators in useful pedagogical judgements and understanding their students

Teacher collaborative knowledge sharing and development interact to enhance student learning. Students will experience more success and growth in their conceptions of language equity if they receive the same messages from teachers across classrooms. Of course, collaborative work and sending a consistent message to students about success should not preclude or limit teachers in their ability to maintain their own unique pedagogical style and address the specific student population in their class. Rather than *technocratic instruction* driven by top-down standardized formal practices that are "teacher-proof," we see the main goal of teacher teams as supporting teachers in adapting instruction to their specific learners. This is known as *adaptive teaching*.

Adaptive teaching adjusts instruction to fit the linguistic, cultural, and instructional strengths of students in a particular classroom and school (Parsons et al., 2018). It emphasizes a commitment to recognizing and promoting students' linguistic resources to support growth and equity (Wineburg et al., 2012). We believe collaborative work should focus on adaptive teaching for two central reasons. First, teachers make multiple decisions in a day about materials, space, content, and how to address an impromptu student question or curiosity. Second, equity means different things in different classrooms for different student populations, with different social histories and dynamics within the school or class (i.e., equity is a dynamic not a static concept) (Kumashiro, 2000). Engaging in equitable language teaching means teachers must constantly investigate and tailor instruction to their unique context. At its core, adaptive teaching is both responsive and affirming. It should respond to the educational, social, political, cultural, and linguistic experiences of students. Equally important, it should take an asset-based approach to pedagogy (see Ladson-Billings's culturally relevant pedagogy, Gay's culturally responsive instruction, and Moll's funds of knowledge) where the multiple identities students bring to the classroom (e.g., their gender, class, race, and nationality) are valued and validated. Before teachers can engage in this kind of adaptive instruction, they need to collectively interrogate their individual and collective understandings around language equity, a process called "professional sensemaking."

Three elements compose *professional sensemaking* (Horn & Campbell, 2015): *pedagogical actions* comprised of intentional and unintentional choices that educators make; *pedagogical reasoning,* sometimes called "instructional reasoning" (Tiilikainen et al., 2019), the rationale or reasons for these actions; and *pedagogical responsibility,* teachers' sense of obligations (moral, ethical, institutional) that so often undergirds reasoning about instruction and actions in the classroom (Chen et al., 2020). We draw on this understanding of professional sensemaking to guide a process of critical teacher inquiry, what we refer to here as, *collaborative professional sensemaking for equitable language teaching.* This kind of professional sensemaking is at the core of teacher collaborations in PLCs.

Collaboration that supports sensemaking around equitable language teaching provides teachers with an opportunity to jointly create a more equitable language environment while still facilitating (a) continued instructional autonomy, (b) flexibility in their text choices and activities across content areas, and (c) creative ways of aligning these practices to other initiatives at the school (e.g., text-dependent reading) or using these routines to augment or subvert existing initiatives while still meeting standards. We focus in this chapter on teachers like Mr. Lesley (6th grade), Ms. Una (7th grade), and Ms. Elmer (8th grade). As these instructors demonstrate, working with colleagues in professional sensemaking teams can bolster equitable language beliefs and adaptive teaching practices by developing continuity and alignment across classrooms, while also supporting the unique characteristics of each classroom.

Planning for Action for the Community

Tips for Team Work on Equitable Language Instruction

- In teams, use structured routines, protocols, or cycles (e.g., frameworks for consuming videos, critiquing lesson plans, or simulations) to support exploration of beliefs, commitments, barriers to implementation, and practices associated with equitable language instruction.
- Share strategies and collaborate to engage in collective adaptive teaching that is responsive and validates the varied social, political, educational, cultural, political, and linguistic identities and experiences of students in your classroom.

- Create a collaborative and reflective space to engage in team activities that promote teachers' instructional choices, reasoning, and responsibility (i.e., professional sensemaking) to equitable language instruction.

Building Collaborative Professional Sensemaking

At the beginning of this chapter, we shared a meeting between Mr. Lesley, Ms. Una, and Ms. Elmer. Their interactions may seem to be predominantly about content and pedagogical planning, but their decisions and interpretations of appropriate practice are rooted in their own beliefs. If we look closely, we can see that these three teachers have divergent understandings of the role of language and language teaching in school. Ms. Una's initial choices about her graphic organizer—to have students write in character names and traits—position language as instrumental for content goals, that is, language is the medium through which content is expressed. Ms. Elmer's feedback to Ms. Una positions language itself as central to study; her recommendations include quotes from the text and analysis of the language use of each character, making students conscious and critical about language choices. Mr. Lesley's comments about the lack of opportunities to practice language conventions see language use as about meeting a prescribed standard and show his concern that not all students are being positioned as skilled language users. These teachers represent a range of common understandings of language, yet not all of these conceptions necessarily lead to equitable language teaching. We see teacher teams as a critical space for professional sensemaking, where teachers can talk about their pedagogical actions, reasoning, and sense of responsibility, and to reflect on these understandings as they relate to linguistic equity and dismantling misconceptions.

Pedagogical Reasoning

The same pedagogical action or decision can be driven by very different reasoning. Teacher teams should develop reasoning that disrupts *monoglossic ideologies,* that is, ways of thinking that focus on one language as correct and conventional (Bakhtin, 1981). Initially, Mr. Lesley pushes Ms. Una to add more opportunities for students to practice language conventions consistent with their state standards, embracing a way of thinking about language that placed standardized English as the gold standard, leading him in the past to often "correct" students in his classroom, asking students to restate their ideas in standardized English during all activities and interactions.

We encourage disrupting monoglossic ideologies in teams with activities that promote the value of multiple languages, dialects, and variations for specific purposes and the power associated with moving consciously between different ways of speaking and presenting ideas. One fruitful collaborative activity is language mapping. *Language mapping,* designed in collaboration with our partner schools, involves a collective exploration of one's varied linguistic resources (Phillips Galloway, Meston, & Dobbs, 2022). The construction of a personal language map asks teachers via prompts to consider the various language communities (Gee, 2012) they participate in based on their geography, culture, shared interests/hobbies, professional interests, academic communities, social spaces, social media, and family spaces (see Figure 6.2 for the mapping template). The prompts encourage teacher teams to consider how each individual in the team learned to use language across their lives and the unique uses of language that come from these different spaces.

In one PLC where teachers completed this activity, they described myriad language communities they belonged to, extending far beyond standardized English. Teachers referenced "being from Eastie" [East Boston], participation in the community of exercise enthusiasts on YouTube, gamers

Figure 6.2. Blank Language Map Template

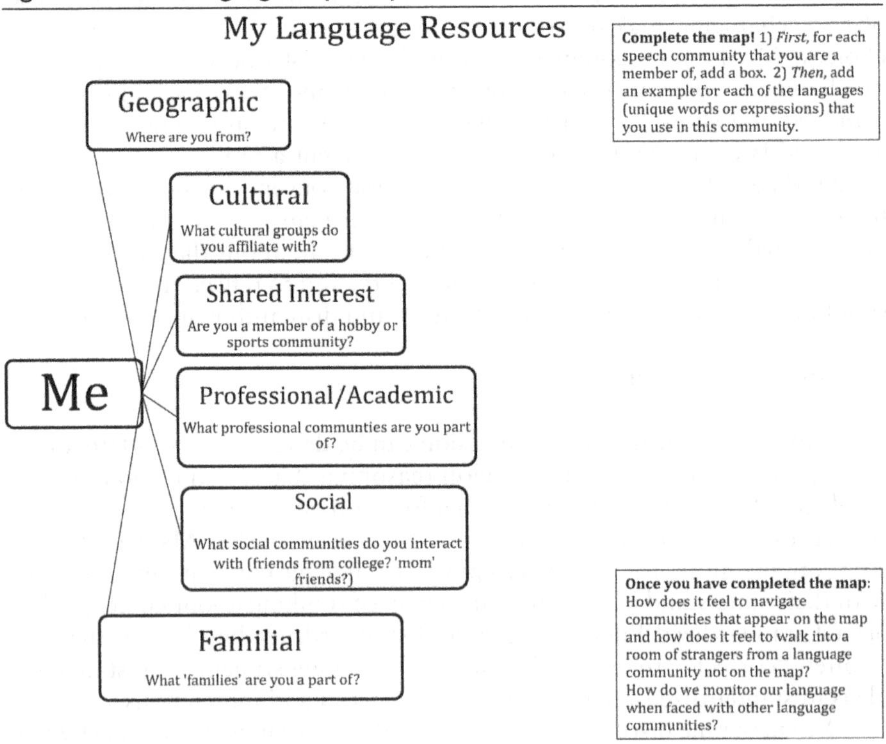

playing an array of different games, and lasting memberships in school communities from K–12 and college. Each of these language communities had particular language use conventions, and teachers in this PLC shared the particular language -isms from various contexts in ways that promoted camaraderie and appreciation of shared and divergent language communities across teachers.

The prompts asked teachers to reflect on how it felt to navigate language communities on and off their map and the ways they monitor their language use across these spaces. These discussions offered a productive space to openly reflect on and identify conceptions of language that promote and limit linguistic equity. Language mapping can help uncover language resources, resituate them as useful across a variety of contexts, and uncover language hierarchies that might already be embraced by participants. For example, Mr. Lesley, a White man from a working-class family, uncovered his many language communities, including a basketball club, and was able to recognize his emphasis on a linguistic standard, despite his own fluid use of various language registers, like language on the basketball court, which made him a socially competent and engaged person. Through this activity, he was able to see how building a variety of language skills is critical to being able to understand the power of language. Mr. Lesley went on to implement this activity in his classroom to show his students the value of various linguistic resources in serving different purposes and the richness of language across context. This activity helped Mr. Lesley debunk, for both himself and his students, a monoglossic approach to language instruction.

Figure 6.3. Teacher Example 1

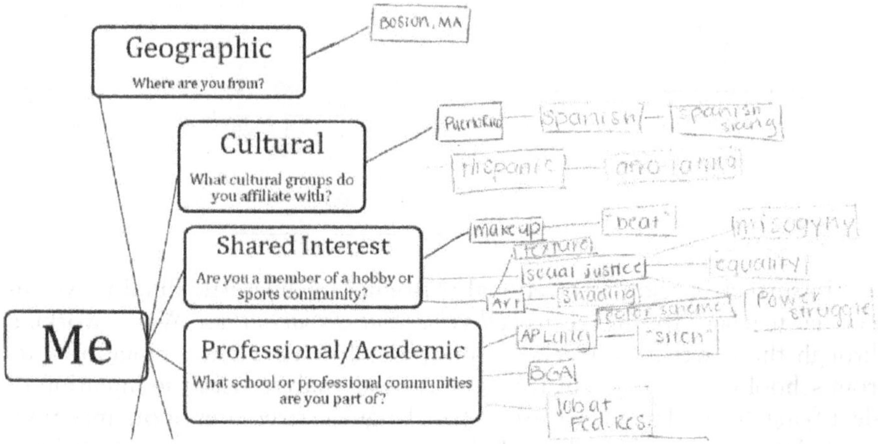

Figure 6.4. Teacher Example 2

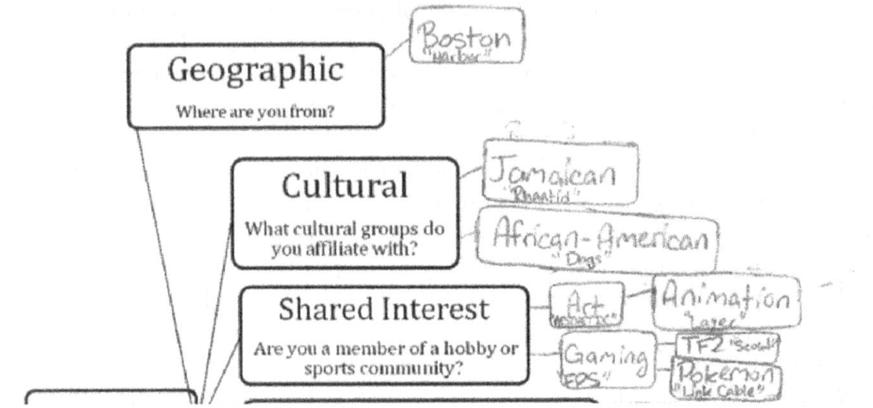

Figure 6.5. Teacher Example 3

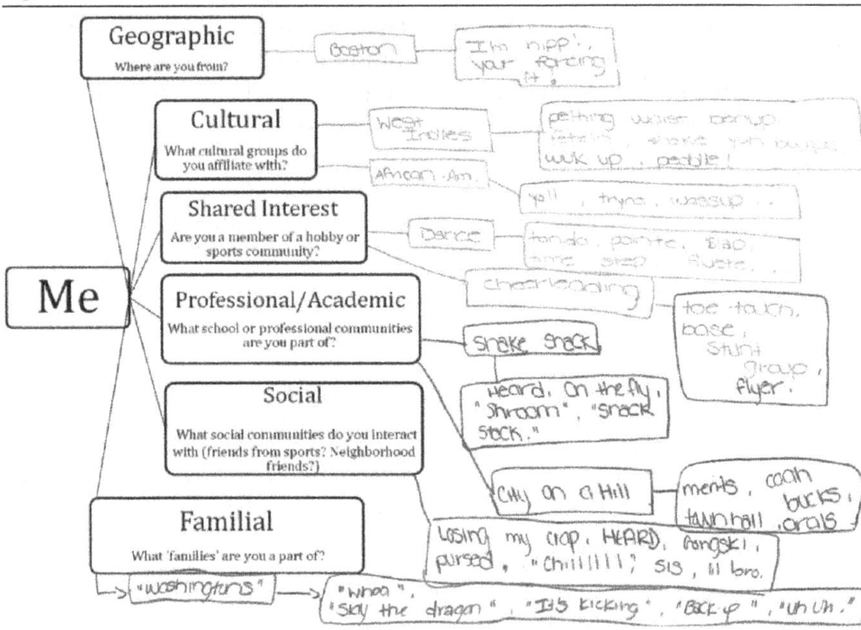

To further develop instructional reasoning for linguistic fluidity, we encourage teachers to engage in *reflective text set activities.* When working through these activities, teacher teams should first review a range of texts from school classrooms that teachers use and analyze with the intention of identifying diverse language features (i.e., language structures or organization, vocabulary, and ways words are linked) and scripts (i.e., language associated with "playing the part" of a historian or mathematician). Teacher teams can also gather texts with different dialectical variants as well as examine features of language used by students in the school. Identifying texts that demonstrate linguistic fluidity—texts that consciously and purposefully move between language from different language contexts and settings—is particularly useful for showcasing the power of different ways of using language to disseminate ideas. We saw several teacher teams work collaboratively to dissect texts being used in classrooms, such as a speech by President Barack Obama and a novel by Toni Morrison, to demonstrate how these texts can accomplish academic purposes, include structures associated with academic texts (such as argumentation or point of view), and also include language features we might associate with English that is not standardized, like language structures and features associated with dialects. These texts also present opportunities to directly interrogate how understandings of language intersect with assumptions about race, class, and gender. For example, both Barack and Michelle Obama are people of color with tremendous wealth, influence, and power, yet their use of dialects was often perceived differently by the media as a function of their gender. Analyzing how writers use their linguistic resources to express themselves and their varied identities, as well as achieve specific purposes, is a key step in unlearning a monoglossic approach to language.

Exploring the ways language varies in different texts within one discipline can also be revealing. For example, in a science PLC, teachers might note differences between the language used in the science textbook versus in a science article for a general audience. When exploring different plant life, like moss, a teacher might contrast sentences from the textbook like, "Mosses commonly grow in large colonies and can appear like green carpet. Moss plants are composed of leafy stalks with rhizoids at their base," with a generalist article about moss with text that reads, "Moss usually appears when the garden conditions are not favorable for growing grass or flowers. The moss is filling in the space where grass will not grow." The language of the textbook may be denser with regard to the number of ideas packed into one sentence, the abstraction of the language, and the emphasis on defining critical terms and plant parts. An article for a general audience will likely have less specialized science vocabulary, sentence structures more similar to speech, and focus on information that is useful to the reader. Similarly, language arts teachers can find variability across the curriculum, in poems, biographies, novels, and narrative nonfiction. Looking across texts in school showcases just how much language variation there is and the importance of being able to notice and analyze language differences without viewing some as better than others.

Teacher teams could also examine texts created by teachers themselves. As individuals, we have unique linguistic styles and preferences. PowerPoint slides, essay prompts, or comments to students all provide an opportunity for teachers to reflect on their own writing style and language use. In one cross-content area team meeting, Ms. Una and Ms. Villarreal were contrasting how they provide feedback on student writing in their 7th-grade English and social studies classes, respectively. They laughed about their own linguistic quirks that derive from spaces outside of school, specifically their social circles. Digging further, they noticed that their comments in the margins of students' papers convey their unique linguistic styles. Ms. Una commented that she continuously writes in the margins when she encourages a student to add another example from the text to bolster their argument: "You got this!" This is a phrase she sees as a spillover from her outside-of-school activities as a long-distance runner, accustomed to screaming this to other runners as they reach the finish line. Ms. Villarreal also noted some patterns in her own comments, particularly her use of "Órale" when students use a novel linguistic element (e.g., metaphor in their writing or language about evidence). She explained that she often writes "Órale, well done!" While Spanish is not spoken by most students in her class, all her students are familiar with "Órale," a common Mexican slang that can be used to express enthusiasm and encouragement. Born and raised in Mexico, Ms. Villarreal often expresses her excitement in her native language and this particular term has caught on in her class, with the students often saying "Orale! Good job!" when a peer does something impressive.

Many of the teachers we have worked with started by assuming there was nothing unique about their own language use, especially if they grew up speaking primarily White Mainstream English, like Ms. Una and Mr. Lesley. Ms. Una, a White teacher from the midwestern United States, described her experience like this:

> I was writing a narrative [as a sample for her class] and saw that a lot of the dialogue that I was making up really was representative of how I actually do speak. For example, my characters were like "Oh, for crying out loud" or "Oh, dear" and that was interesting to see in my own writing. It was kind of bringing to life my own background and my own way of communicating.

Another fairly new teacher in their grade-level team, Ms. Early, described her experience using Black English language as follows:

> Recognizing in my own writing the richness of my own dialect, especially being from the South and being Black and specifically from Atlanta . . . I think recognizing the, how do I say it, the specialness of how we say things has been making me challenge the way we were taught not to say things. Because I think there's like a richness of storytelling, especially with AAVE [African American Vernacular English]. So, I think that has been making me unlearn what I thought was supposed to be just so.

A close and careful exploration of the language within individual texts, in a given discipline, across content area texts, and for writers with different backgrounds can help advance the understanding of linguistic fluidity and variation through collaborative, inquiry-focused conversations.

Pedagogical Responsibility

Teachers' sense of moral, ethical, and institutional obligation to linguistic equity is critical for equitable language teaching. To bolster pedagogical responsibility that undergirds action, we believe teams should continually use team meetings as spaces to reflect on language hierarchies and how they have come to influence their instruction and evaluation of their students. These reflective discussions should occur continuously, not just as part of an isolated activity or event. Teams should create a space to regularly "check in." As an example, we encourage teachers to continually explore their own language when talking about students and student growth, whether that is by capturing and analyzing videos of teaching, meeting notes, artifacts in the school and/or on school websites, as well as real-time monitoring of the language used to describe students', teachers', and administrators' work.

As an opportunity to hone language-awareness vigilance, we present the words of teachers from a cohort, or grade-level, meeting where teachers met across content areas to talk about student data and performance. As you read these quotes, think about whether they support linguistic hierarchies and linguicism or, alternatively, linguistic equity. We encourage readers to try to break down implicit assumptions in these statements about what student success is, how practicing language conventions is different than dissecting or critiquing them, and what assumptions are embedded in the idea of so-called proper and accurate speaking and learning.

> His contributions make things chaotic. Students need to be able to understand using evidence and language from the text. He does not have the language needed to be successful. (Teacher 1, 6th-grade social studies)

> I am worried about her. She needs to be using academic language, not the everyday language that one uses in conversation. I know this takes longer to acquire in the classroom environment and should be folded into daily lessons. I am giving students the opportunity to practice school language using different modalities daily. (Teacher 2, 6th-grade science)

> I am trying not to make them feel any different from the rest of the class; I need to accurately help them in talking properly in class. (Teacher 3, 6th-grade ELA)

In Figure 6.6, we list discussion questions that can be posed in teams to explore these quotes and how they may undermine or inhibit a commitment to linguistic equity.

Figure 6.6. Analyzing Teacher Talk to Support Pedagogical Responsibility

Teacher Context	Teacher Quote	Discussion Questions
Teacher, 6th-grade social studies	"His contributions make things chaotic. Students need to be able to understand using evidence and language from the text. He does not have the language needed to be successful."	How is success being defined here? How do you see this definition in the teacher's words?
Teacher 2, 6th-grade science	"I am worried about her. She needs to be using academic language, not the everyday language that one uses in conversation. I know this takes longer to acquire in the classroom environment and should be folded into daily lessons. I am giving students the opportunity to practice school language using different modalities daily."	Is everyday language really so divergent from the language of academic tasks? If so, how and why does this difference matter for meaning-making? Are different modalities going to support language awareness? Why or why not?
Teacher 3, 6th-grade ELA	"I am trying not to make them feel any different from the rest of the class; I need to accurately help them in talking properly in class."	Is being different problematic? Why or under what conditions is it problematic? What does it mean to talk properly? How is this teacher inadvertently supporting language hierarchies in this response?

These questions are intended to support teachers in reframing the tensions raised in the quotes and suggest equity-centered approaches to addressing these language dilemmas. For example, in the case of the 6th-grade social studies teacher who feels frustrated by a student's "chaotic" comments, the teacher could take an alternative approach to viewing student contributions and see even these contributions as instructionally productive. Specially, they could encourage varied contributions and accompany these contributions with ways of restating them in different forms depending on the academic purpose. A discussion of the differences between phrasing can facilitate rich discussions about how language is used in particular ways for specific audiences and the implications of those choices for including or excluding different participants.

Similarly, the 6th-grade science teacher who worries about her student's use of colloquial language might also take an alternative approach and instead of viewing this student with concern, might see this student's language use as providing an opportunity to engage the class in a discussion of diverse language resources. This same teacher can draw upon the content of this student's contributions and use the unique linguistic choices of this student as a springboard for a language-awareness inquiry routine conversation.

An alternative approach is also possible and important in the case of the 6th-grade ELA teacher who doesn't want her language-minoritized students to feel different from their peers and thus advocates for assimilating them to standardized English. If this teacher started to view all languages as valuable in their own right and focused on linguistic fluidity as the goal, then the differences between students' linguistic stores of knowledge could enrich the classroom and the classroom content as opposed to marginalize some students in the class.

Pedagogical responsibility asks that teachers dismantle misconceptions and support conceptions of language that promote equitable language teaching. As part of this process, teachers should explore their own conceptions and misconceptions through repeated questioning during team meetings that focus on supporting linguistic fluidity and not a linguistic standard. To interrupt the kinds of misconceptions about language prevalent in the quotes in Figure 6.6, we encourage teachers to periodically ask the following questions as they talk about students and families and review student work samples and student performance:

1. How can we promote student language knowledge in and out of school?
2. How can we shift the conversation to being about supporting linguistic fluidity and not language "accuracy" or "proper language" use for students and teachers?
3. How do our own experiences of language teaching inform our conceptions of the value of linguistic fluidity?
4. Can we describe students' ability to share what they know in ways that focus on developing versatility rather than standardized language?

These questions provide a space for complex discussions about language and build a sense of ethical, moral, and institutional responsibility to equitable language teaching. In response to the question, "How do our own experiences of language teaching inform our conceptions of the value of linguistic fluidity?" Ms. Elmer, a Black woman originally from the urban South of the United States, described her memories of growing up in a predominantly Black community and reflected on the messages she got about her own use of Black English language:

> Well, I went to a predominantly Black school growing up. I grew up in East Atlanta, so that's like DeKalb County. And because we were a predominantly Black population, it was like, the way that we spoke was policed a lot. So it was like, this is good, this is bad. Don't say this, say it like this. . . . It was actually funny, because I rarely had White teachers growing up. So, it was definitely from older Black people who were telling you that.

In response to these prompts, she explained that her views about her language resources were handed down to her, that is, the Black educators who taught her had experienced linguistic discrimination and prejudice, and as a result, focused on supporting their own Black students in using standardized English to reduce marginalization. To support her students in seeing language differently, she aims to center language in all her teaching and specifically to support linguistic fluidity so they feel empowered to share their voice regardless of the language they choose to use. This conversation helped Mr. Lesley to realize that, like Ms. Elmer's teachers, he was worried about students' use of standardized English above all else.

Another example from this same school occurred in the grade-level meeting for the 6th grade to discuss a student named Elvira. Elvira's math teacher, Mr. Evans, a White monolingual teacher from a rural town in the Northeast, brought to the meeting student work from a warmup activity, a quick writing exercise in which students had to jot down what they "Notice and Wonder" about a linear graph on the board. Elvira's write-up of what she noticed about the graph showing a linear relationship between the temperature outside and ice cream consumption read "dots in the graph, and the maximum 110." Initially the discussion centered on Mr. Lesley's concern about Elvira's "limited language abilities." He argued that this writing sample showed "very little language and not in full sentences." He suggested to Mr. Evans that he use sentence starters to help Elvira write in grammatically correct sentences. However, using and exploring the four prompts we previously listed, this group of teachers, including Mr. Lesley, began to discuss this student work sample in different ways. In exploring Elvira's work using the prompt "Can we describe students' ability to share what they know in ways that focus on developing versatility rather than standardized language?" the conversation shifted considerably, as did the pedagogical suggestions. Mr. Evans explained that he asked Elvira about her write-up, and she explained that she was curious if the dots represented real data points. He quoted her as saying "Are these dots real true hot days and people got ice cream on that day, because where was it 110 degrees?" He explained that her elaboration showed that she was engaging in important mathematical thinking about how information can be graphed, with graphs and linear relationships sometimes showing averages or extrapolating beyond specific data points to plot a relationship (i.e., 110 degrees might not represent an actual temperature that occurred). Mr. Evans explained that this back-and-forth exchange showed that Elvira was engaging in thoughtful mathematical thinking, noticing, and language. For example, he highlighted her description of a specific data point that seemed out of the appropriate range (110 degrees is really hot for the Northeast!).

Mr. Evans revised Mr. Lesley's suggestion to just include sentence starters to be more adaptive and responsive, highlighting and bolstering Elvira's existing language use. He proposed drawing attention to her use of evidence to explain her developing hypothesis that the dots on the linear line might not represent specific days in their city but instead might represent averages across the country or extrapolations. She used the word "maximum" in her response, and he wanted to talk further with her about why that maximum mattered and help her elaborate on this in writing. He proposed that he provide sentence starters—like Mr. Lesley suggested—but he would also accompany these starters with questions, asking Elvira to talk with him about which starters made the most sense for communicating her ideas and her evidence and why the current response might not capture the wealth of information she communicated in her verbal response. The teacher team shifted from talking about the limits of Elvira's language to how instruction can be adaptive and focus on the myriad ways language can be used to showcase ideas and explicit ways to draw students' attention to these functions and ways to use language for learning. The beliefs and understandings that inform teacher reasoning and responsibility directly translate to teacher practice and the ability of educators to take up equitable language teaching in earnest.

Pedagogical Action

To understand how pedagogical reasoning and responsibility can be applied to action for equitable language teaching, we again return to Mr. Lesley, Ms. Una, and Ms. Elmer. Each teacher is using a different, grade appropriate text, but they all are planning their lessons using the framework of language-awareness inquiry routines that uses a questioning process to draw students' attention to language features, purposes, and power that support content learning. Each teacher is developing transformational prompts—questions that reveal how language is associated with power, privilege, and belonging—and metalinguistic prompts—questions that help students attend to and manipulate language for distinct purposes. These two types of prompts rely on sturdy pedagogical reasoning and responsibility to equity.

Both Ms. Una and Mr. Lesley are talking about the two texts they have introduced to students: *Roll of Thunder, Hear My Cry* and *Number the Stars,* respectively. *Roll of Thunder, Hear My Cry* describes the experience of the Logans, a Black family in Mississippi in 1933, and their struggle to maintain their farmland in the context of racism, segregation, and local lynchings. The book is narrated by the 9-year-old daughter. *Number the Stars* describes a friendship between two girls—one Jewish and one not—in Copenhagen, Denmark, in 1943 during the Nazi occupation. The story follows the 10-year-old protagonist as she rescues her Jewish friend and participates in the Danish resistance. Before engaging in discussions about the text, they provided students with some background knowledge about the periods and settings for each book, as well as core concepts that will be critical for students to understand as they explore themes of injustice and power.

Both teachers are eager to address the craft of the authors as well as the language unique to these texts. They are co-planning lessons where they will dig into the language being used in their unique texts to support students' linguistic fluidity. Ms. Una is eager to highlight the language of the main character and narrator, Cassie, in *Roll of Thunder, Hear My Cry* and how her unique voice and use of language as a Black girl in the rural South influences the reader's experience of the book. Mr. Lesley is excited to show how the author of *Number the Stars* uses language to create suspense, fear, and disorientation. Both teachers are trying to hone their students' skills in analyzing text for meaning. However, the prompts they use can either direct attention to language in ways that promote linguistic equity or limit linguistic equity. In sync with their school's new initiative focused on text-dependent questions, both teachers have selected several passages from the text to examine in detail and both intend to engage in multiple discussions in their classes about the content in the first chapters.

Both teachers used prompts associated with both transformational aims (which focus on uncovering injustice) and metalinguistic aims (which focus on linguistic choices and features) to help promote students' critical consciousness about language and power. These aims will carry across multiple lessons, and both teachers have already flagged places in subsequent chapters to return to these questions that underscore how language and power are intertwined. Initially, Mr. Lesley's transformational aim was to focus on who is using what language and when with the associated prompt, "Does it matter that the Germans speak Dutch poorly?" But using teacher team discussion prompts, Ms. Una pushed Mr. Lesley and asked him to think about whether his prompt:

- Critiques the role of disciplinary scripts—that is, the way language is prescribed by a disciplinary community or community of power over knowledge
- Highlights the ways in which power is instantiated and maintained

Ms. Una's questions provided Mr. Lesley with a space to dissect his own pedagogical reasoning and sense of responsibility to equity. Based on these questions, he revised his prompts to be more closely aligned with helping students critically evaluate the relationship between language and power (i.e., "The soldiers speak German, and the main characters speak Dutch;

how does language use make us powerful or vulnerable?"). This improved prompt provided Mr. Lesley with an opportunity to be consistent in the way he talks about power and resistance when discussing the content of the book. He can also use this revised prompt to talk about the relationship between language and power in the world more broadly, not just in Denmark during this period. In addition, he is drawing students' attention to the disciplinary scripts of ELA and their focus on the human experience and language that evokes emotion.

Ms. Una, meanwhile, benefited from Mr. Lesley's feedback. She was excited about discussing the different traits and motivations of the characters in one chapter of *Roll of Thunder, Hear My Cry*. She initially began with the question, "What language shows us how these characters are different?" However, when she piloted this with a small group of students in her afterschool reading group, they ended up focusing on words like "wicked" or calling characters "naughty." As she shared with Mr. Lesley, the students immediately took the perspective of the teacher in the story, who does view the acts of the protagonist and her brother as naughty, and the narrator, who viewed the other children as bothersome. Ms. Una knew she wanted the students to focus on more descriptive language that captures characters' struggle, power relationships, and feelings of anger rather than whether characters are good or bad. Mr. Lesley worked with Ms. Una to discuss how they might reframe the question to facilitate a focus on vocabulary that captures power struggles, the feelings of the characters, and the ways in which they show their frustrations. They also wanted to consider this tension about whose perspective to attend to: the perspective of children or the perspective of adults. Mr. Lesley used teacher team discussion prompts to push Ms. Una by asking her to think about whether her metalinguistic aim and metalinguistic prompts:

- Improved students' ability to reflect on and manipulate the structural features of language in particular contexts?
- Uncovered linguistic injustice and/or the power of linguistic fluidity?
- Made visible how language is used in similar ways and in different ways across disciplinary communities?

As a result of their conversation, Ms. Una changed her overarching metalinguistic question to focus more on language related to injustice and power in the chapter. She asked, "How is the theme of injustice and power shown in the idioms and language used in this chapter?" In so doing, she was better able to highlight different perspectives (teachers versus children), salient character traits, and how power or lack of power is demonstrated in verbs as opposed to labels describing the children. This revised question also aligns with Ms. Una's transformational aim and associated prompt ("How does the Black English language or dialect in this work influence how we understand the experience of this young Black girl?") and her ongoing discussion about how the dialect of the main character and family is critical to the book's message about empowerment. See Figure 6.7, which presents Ms. Una's and Mr. Lesley's lesson planning using language-awareness inquiry routine prompts.

Figure 6.7. Planning Language Awareness Inquiry Routines in ELA Classrooms Using Texts Commonly Included in Middle Grade Curriculum

Overarching Prompts	
Transformational Script Prompts	
Number the Stars	The soldiers speak German, and the main characters speak Dutch; how does language use make us powerful or vulnerable?
Roll of Thunder, Hear My Cry	How does the Black language or dialect in this work influence how we understand the experience of this young Black girl?
Metalinguistic Script Prompts	
Number the Stars	How does the author use language to help us understand the fear of the characters? How does the author use language to show differences between then and now?
Roll of Thunder, Hear My Cry	How are the themes of injustice and power shown in the idioms and language used in this chapter?
Language Features	
Discourse	
Number the Stars	How does the author use language to show the power of the soldiers?
Roll of Thunder, Hear my Cry	How is the language of the teachers different than the language of the children? How is authority being communicated in these different ways?
Vocabulary	
Number the Stars	"civilized," "hoodlums," "obstinate," "impassive"
Roll of Thunder, Hear my Cry	"jammed," "thrust," "maverick," "imprisoned freedom," "indignant anger/indignation"
Syntax	
Number the Stars	"'She glanced through the window, down to the street corner *where* the soldiers stood, their faces impassive beneath the metal helmets.'"
	"For Kristi, the soldiers were simply part of the landscape, something that had always been there, on every corner, as unimportant as lampposts, *throughout* her remembered life."
Roll of Thunder, Hear my Cry	"'You *ain't* never had to live in nobody's place but your own.'" "'Yes, *ain't* that something.'"

We encourage teams to ask these questions as they co-plan. This collaborative approach can surface pedagogical reasoning and promote pedagogical responsibility to equitable language teaching. As they review each other's language-awareness lesson plans, teachers should ask:

Do your transformational prompts . . .

- critique the role of disciplinary scripts, that is, the way language is prescribed by a disciplinary community or community of power over knowledge?
- highlight the ways in which power is instantiated and maintained through language?

Do your metalinguistic prompts . . .

- improve students' ability to reflect on and manipulate the structural features of language in particular contexts?
- uncover linguistic injustice and/or the power of linguistic fluidity?
- make visible how language is used in similar ways and in different ways across disciplinary communities?

While teachers should prepare initial prompts (transformative and metalinguistic) intended to set off a cascade of back-and-forth exchanges, some of the most fruitful conversations and discussions in classrooms happen organically in relationship to students' subsequent questions and comments. Thus, our aim here is to provide a framework for discussions that will set teachers up for success in engaging in adaptive instruction that supports equitable language teaching.

Planning for Action for the Community

Tips for Collaborative Professional Sensemaking Activities to Support Equitable Language Instruction

- Language Mapping Activity to self-reflect on personal conceptions and misconceptions of language to reveal the important role of linguistic fluidity in everyday interactions.
- Reflective Text Set Activities to showcase how linguistic variation is always present within individual texts, in each discipline, across content area texts, and for writers with different backgrounds and highlight the benefits of teaching for linguistic fluidity.

- Reflective and Reframing Discussion Prompts for teachers to examine through repeated collective questioning and analysis of their talk, artifacts, and behaviors their values and commitment to supporting linguistic fluidity and not a linguistic standard.
- Co-Planning Prompts for Language Awareness Inquiry Routines to support a framework for pedagogical conversations that center equitable language teaching for student success and promote professional reasoning and responsibility toward linguistic equity.

FORMING TEAMS

We have laid out high-efficacy practices for teaming and specific goals and activities teams can engage in to create a space for collaborative professional reasoning, responsibility, and action that support equitable language teaching. To begin this work, schools should either make use of existing teams or create new teams that can collaborate well together. The next section outlines how you might get started on forming effective teams.

In many schools where teacher teams are successful, it is common to have both an academic content team of subject-area teachers and a student cohort team of grade-level teachers across subject areas. Both sets of teams can address curricular decisions, planning, student assessment data and information, as well as aspects of the school climate (Moore-Johnson, 2019). We believe that both of these types of teams have a role to play in supporting the beliefs, principles, and practices of equitable language teaching. Our work with teachers, many of whom are highlighted in this text, shows that schools are organized in very different ways. Subsequently, we recognize that the structure of school teams may vary tremendously. It is at the discretion of schools to decide whether continued planning and discussion of language-awareness inquiry routines and equitable language teaching beliefs should be led by grade-level teams, content-area teams, both, or some other formulation based on the unique organization of each school.

COLLABORATING WITH COLLEAGUES WHO FOCUS ON A SIMILAR CONTENT AREA

"Same-work" teams, or teams that share a similar subject-area focus, allow teachers to collaborate in meaningful ways about shared curriculum and types of textual materials. To determine whether "same work" teams may be particularly fruitful in your school, we encourage school sites to examine the following questions:

- Do teachers in your building already have time set up in the schedule to meet in same-work teams? Do they have shared space, such as workrooms, that could be used for meetings or other structural supports?
- Is there a schoolwide focus on improving student success in particular content areas that might facilitate the seamless integration of discussions of equitable language teaching?
- Are you using new curricula that is still being learned where equitable language teaching principles can be discussed? Or, making large-scale change to disciplinary curricula that already exist?
- Are there teachers in same-work teams that already trust one another and would feel comfortable exploring complex beliefs about language together?

If the answer to any of these questions is yes, then same-work teams might be a good space for exploring beliefs and practices associated with equitable language teaching and linguistic fluidity. These configurations can lead to deep collaborations for participants as they carefully explore their content work in a focused way. Same-work teams also tend to already have more structural support (as structures like grade-level teams or common planning time already exist in many schools). Same-work teams provide useful opportunities for teachers to align their equitable language teaching practices across grades. As described in Chapter 5, language-awareness inquiry routines can be used at all grade levels. Same-work teams can facilitate a developmental approach, where teachers are using these same routines over time and continuously building a muscle around content-specific language awareness and equity.

COLLABORATING WITH COLLEAGUES ACROSS THE GRADE LEVEL

Collaborative work can also productively occur among teachers who focus on different content areas. Sometimes content teachers collaborate across different subjects, either because those teachers teach all subjects, or because teams are formed from teachers who all specialize in different content area work across a grade level. When teams get together to collaborate about students at the grade level, it is possible to have deep and comprehensive discussion about student language patterns across the various content areas students are engaged with in any given school year. Elementary teachers who teach multiple subjects across the day, middle school teachers who teach more than one topic, and teachers who serve a specific school population (e.g., students receiving special education services or multilingual students receiving TESOL instruction) can identify patterns and variation in student language use across a day. To determine whether cross-content teams may be well suited for collaboration about equitable language teaching practices, we encourage school sites to consider the following questions:

- Are there existing structures like grade-level teams that might be used to build a collaborative learning space?
- Do teachers across areas meet to discuss consistency and divergence in student work across diverse contexts?
- Does the unique content expertise of teachers in this group facilitate a safe space for discussion of diverse perspectives and beliefs?
- Is there a need to build a stronger culture around equitable language teaching practices across the whole school building?

If the answer to any of these questions is yes, then cross-content teams may be a fruitful context for supporting equitable language teaching beliefs and practices. These cross-content groupings can lead to greater interdisciplinary understandings of language and strong relationship-building among teachers who might not have other reasons to collaborate in more traditional professional learning structures like workshops. Developing linguistic fluidity supports the exploration of various conventions of different language communities, which is most evident in cross-content area teams. For teachers and their colleagues who are hoping to make connections among different content areas, or to make their work more interdisciplinary and more fluid in using language from classroom to classroom, cross-content area teams can be an excellent platform to make these instructional changes.

* * *

Teacher teams can work together to develop pedagogical reasoning, consider pedagogical responsibility, and enact pedagogical actions that support equitable language teaching. The activities and exploratory discussion prompts described in this chapter help teachers collaboratively reflect on and adapt teaching and learning to their unique population of students. Through collaboration, teachers can work together to develop their own professional sensemaking and, in turn, support linguistic fluidity in their students. Classroom teaching does not occur in a bubble. Instead, educators need to think and act collectively and in coordination to best serve their students and communities. Effective teacher teams are necessary for creating more equitable, linguistically permeable spaces.

CHAPTER 6 CLOSING REFLECTION

Now that you have learned about teamwork and collaboration as a key lever for addressing misconceptions about language and promoting equitable language teaching, what are some ways you might advocate for these types of collaborations focused on professional sensemaking in your school? Who might you want to work with to do this work? And how might you use the explorations described here with your team to support dismantling of language hierarchies and replacing them with a focus on linguistic fluidity?

Taking a Systemic Approach: Improving School Culture Through Collective Inquiry

> **Conceptions That Promote Equitable Language Teaching**
>
> It is not enough for individual teachers to support equitable language teaching. Instead, educators, leaders, and families must partner to collectively address structures and systems within schools and beyond them to reimagine and enact more just language use in schools.

Towering Hill School, an urban elementary and middle school in the midwestern United States, has become known throughout the state for its activism around language equity and its culture of equitable teaching and learning. There are visual representations of this culture all over the school with multilingual posters and flags hung in classrooms and hallways and diverse languages on the school's website. Administrators, teachers, parents, and students alike feel welcome to use multiple linguistic resources. Classroom observations consistently highlight language and linguistic fluidity as a core feature of instruction and student engagement. Teacher team meetings reflect a continued commitment to linguistic equity in planning, action, and the evaluation of teaching and learning. But Towering Hill School was not always a beacon of equitable language teaching. It is only in the last 10 years that the school has embarked on this important journey to make their school a more linguistically equitable place.

Towering Hill's culture and dedication to language equity did not happen by accident, but instead is the result of a group effort to ensure that equitable language teaching is at the core of everyday organizational structures, daily practice, and interpersonal dynamics. We focus on the school as a whole system, including vertical (e.g., principal to teacher) as well as horizontal (e.g., teacher to teacher) relationships, because injustice is commonly perpetuated through structures and organizational systems as well as in interpersonal interactions, and dismantling these dynamic systems requires a multidirectional and expansive approach (Bonilla-Silva, 2015; Lewis &

Diamond, 2015). A community-wide focus on equity permeates a school's culture. Consistent with work by Ishimaru and colleagues (2022), we argue that equitable language teaching practice should be the "throughline" for changing the school culture at multiple levels. Focusing solely on individual beliefs and bias or practice in a single classroom will not alter organizational and structural dynamics that create and reproduce injustices. Instead, a coordinated, iterative, and multidirectional commitment to knowledge building around equitable language instruction is essential.

A collective inquiry approach that connects educational stakeholders in meaningful ways to equitable language practices at multiple levels is critical. Collective inquiry focuses on exploring how language teaching and learning are enacted currently at the classroom, school, and district level and how they might be reimagined. We focus on collective inquiry in schools to better understand what must be learned, changed, and built to support classroom-, school-, and district-level action and coordination for linguistic equity.

CHAPTER 7 REFLECTION

Take a moment to reflect on the school where you work or one where you have spent time. What might an outsider notice about the school's approach to language in the visual representations at the school? What about professional development work or the ways in which teachers communicate with each other and students about the role of language in learning? Is there one consistent approach to language learning, or do teachers take their own approach? What do administrators communicate about the importance (or lack thereof) of consistency across classrooms? What do you think students might say if you asked them about the school culture around language? Now, imagine your district. What messages about language are conveyed in policies and curricular choices at the district level?

CREATING A SCHOOLWIDE CULTURE OF LINGUISTIC EQUITY

School culture—the values and norms at a school (Hoy, 1990; Heck & Marcoulides, 1996)—is critical to the way language is perceived by students, teachers, and administrators. While school culture can be instantiated in tangible ways (through curricula, resources, or materials), it also pervades intangible facets of a school (like systems, structures, and relationships). Towering Hill School has a school culture that embraces multiple linguistic resources. Visually, this value is seen in the flags in the hallway representing the home cultures of the many students who attend the school, the individual flags outside teachers' doors to represent the students' countries of origin, and signs that denote the languages students know and use.

Posters of the books students are currently reading show protagonists and authors from diverse language backgrounds. There are color-coded labels in several languages on common items in the building so that students know that, for example, purple labels are in Vietnamese, red are in Spanish, green are in English, and orange are in American Sign Language. Handouts on the welcome counter outside the main office appear in many languages. When you listen to the daily announcements, speakers (both adults and students) use a range of language resources to discuss an upcoming play, the theme of a school dance, and deadlines for permission slips for an upcoming 8th-grade trip. The message is that all language is welcome.

By contrast, the culture at Grey Gardens, a school serving students in 5th–8th grade two miles away, is focused on "appropriateness" and speaking in ways that are "proper" and "clear." The chiseled stone monument at the front entry describes the goals for every graduate. The first is that every graduate of the school would have a strong command of "Standard English." This is followed by other goals that emphasize "Standard English" as a priority and the aim that students will act and speak "properly." By focusing on a linguistic standard, Grey Gardens positions their values in direct contrast to Towering Hill School, where the messaging is about linguistic fluidity, and how school community members (administrators, teachers, and students) can use language dynamically to learn and grow. The halls at Grey Gardens are predominately covered with signs that list classroom and school norms around safe and respectful behaviors and posters about school sports events. It is rare to hear students communicate with teachers and administrators using language resources mastered in outside-of-school settings. We provide suggestions throughout this chapter for how schools can and should create cultures that are hospitable to and promote language learning and linguistic equity, and equally important, we argue that these two aims are intertwined. We contend that this involves learning about your school's culture around language teaching, changing practices that might hinder equitable language teaching, and building structures and processes that center both language learning and linguistic equity.

Schools that create equity-centered cultures most effectively do so at multiple levels, supporting students, teachers, and all members of a school community in approaching language thoughtfully. We encourage schools to conduct this work by engaging in *collective inquiry* that addresses *what must be learned* about the school culture around language, *what must be changed* about the school culture around language, and *what must be built* to support a culture of equitable language teaching. This collective inquiry into the culture around language and the generation of next steps for permeating equitable language teaching practices throughout the school system is about exploring structures, organization systems, and relationships that can promote or hinder equitable language teaching.

Equity work begins by carefully examining existing systems in the service of dismantling unjust structures and empowering new equity-oriented visions for the future. Throughout this book we have followed this approach, using language-awareness inquiry (both personal and classroom) as a central practice. When exploring individual beliefs and classroom practice, we promoted an inquiry-based approach to examine language use, explore its *linguistic features,* and interrogate its *power dynamics*. Here, we ask educational stakeholders to take a similar approach that centers reflection and interrogation of language beliefs and practices to unpack the school features (systems, organizational structure, and relationships) that uphold or break down hegemonic and monoglossic approaches to language teaching and create or prevent equitable language teaching at scale. We see administrators as critical to supporting a culture of equitable language teaching. Administrators bring a bird's-eye view of both the school and district and thus are able to partner with educators to identify aspects of the collective culture that might be preventing linguistically equitable classrooms. Administrators set the stage for teachers to develop critical language self-awareness and are central to creating a school environment that interrogates systems of oppression, affirms multiple student identities, and supports community advocacy (Khalifa et al., 2016).

Collective Inquiry: Learning, Changing, and Building

To engage in collective inquiry, schools must create structures and processes that work synergistically to support equitable language teaching. *Structures* are tangible, concrete, and are fundamental to promoting or hindering equitable language teaching (Lesaux et al., 2016). Administrators can create professional learning communities, set aside dedicated time in teachers' schedules during the school day for collective reflection on the linguistic climate, or convene a team of stakeholders to systematically select curriculum and assessments that reify linguistic pluralism. Each of these initiatives—a professional learning community, a weekly time dedicated to meeting, or a curriculum committee—is simply a structure. But in and of themselves, they do not lead to meaningful change. Instead, it is *processes* occurring within these structures, or the interactions and activities of the participants, that create continuous learning and improvement (Lesaux et al., 2016).

To explore and shift a culture around language, schools must look holistically at the structures and processes already in place, those that need to be changed, and those that need to be built. We present three phases of collective inquiry and suggestions for structures and processes that can transform school cultures. The first phase of collective inquiry focuses on learning or examining current practices and involves an *equitable language teaching school culture study*. Before a school can reimagine a new language environment, it needs to learn about its existing culture around language and instruction. The second phase of collective inquiry focuses on areas for change and ways school stakeholders can work together to conceptualize and develop areas for growth. This step involves vulnerability. Working with peers to conceptualize change and engage in discussions around professional reasoning, responsibility, and action for equity requires that educational stakeholders acknowledge their own beliefs and, in most cases, change their practice (Miesner et al., 2022). The final stage of collective inquiry focuses on what must be built, and specifically how to work towards the schools' vision for equitable language teaching. Distinct from the previous phase focused on educational stakeholders collaboratively conceptualizing areas for change, the building phase focuses on community action. This final phase can be challenging as it involves the personal and professional risk taking that comes with trying something new. However, disrupting existing patterns is critical for forging paths to equitable language instruction.

PLANNING FOR ACTION FOR THE COMMUNITY

Tips for All Phases

To productively engage in these three phases, it helps to disaggregate what are the structures and what are the processes that will forward these efforts at each phase.

- Structures are the tangible and concrete aspects of organizing for change. These structures may refer to the professional learning communities established at a school site, to the planning time set aside each week, or to the protocols adopted to guide reform efforts. Structures are easily put into place at school sites and serve as recognizable manifestations of effort and activity; however, structures are often inadequate for creating change without effective processes. To identify productive structures, you might ask: "What are the tangible elements of our efforts? Do we have structures (e.g., existing teams, professional learning communities, training protocols) that will facilitate productive reflection and change?"
- Processes are the activities and interactions of participants within a structure. These processes are fundamental to making structures "work," but we rarely investigate this aspect of our efforts. Processes are often less visible and so we must ask a set of questions to identify them: "What is taking place in the structures we currently have in place (e.g., teams, professional learning communities) that makes them effective? How are we using our planning block or schoolwide meetings to maximize our efforts?"

Phase 1: Examination

To explore what must be learned about the existing culture of a school system, your school's educational stakeholders can conduct an equitable language teaching "school culture study" of the instructional practices and culture around language at a school.

First, assemble a collaborative team to collect artifacts that might indicate your school's approach to language (see Dobbs et al., 2017). It is important that this team include varied stakeholders. Members of your school community should feel represented and stakeholders should support different roles and responsibilities. School leaders (e.g., principals, assistant principals, literacy specialists, PLC leaders) should participate in this work alongside teachers to support an overarching alignment across classrooms and set up the possibility of lasting culture change (see Hallinger & Heck, 2011 and Fullan, 2001). School leaders should also make sure to frame this endeavor as a form of collective inquiry and not an evaluative exercise. The goal is to understand the current schoolwide culture, not individual behaviors or actions.

Next, the team will collect artifacts and data to see the language practices currently in place. Keep in mind the ways teaching approaches and the culture around language are both linked to school, district, and state policies and ideologies as well as broader sociocultural factors (Skrla et al., 2004). Given the systemic nature of factors that limit language equity, the school culture study may cast a wide net, exploring elements of culture beyond the day-to-day teaching in classrooms (Figure 7.1, column 1). The collection and examination of relevant school data should include collecting student work, observing classroom and other school spaces, and consuming information presented to the public by the school, (e.g., the school website) that captures how the school presents itself to the world. Policy documents, curricular resources, assessments, and professional learning materials that come from the district or state and impact views of language and its instruction within a school also offer useful data for analysis by the team.

The school culture study team should describe their work to the school community members and emphasize that they will be collecting as much information as possible, and that the data collected will not be used for evaluative purposes but simply as a means of understanding the current culture around language. It should be emphasized that the school culture study is to explore the culture of the school as a whole, rather than to focus on any individual community members. Building a sense of trust for community members is a key to ensuring the success of improvement efforts (Edmonson, 2018). Once data are collected, the next step is to collaboratively make sense of what was learned using similar questions to those posed in Figure 7.1. Teams should use these questions as a springboard for discussion. And, from these discussions, school sites should have a clear conception of both the formal and informal ways in which the culture around language is shaped.

We recommend that teams set clear parameters for having discussions around school artifacts and data in a way that remains factual and positive, ensuring that all community members feel valued and not judged by the process. It becomes much harder to shift school culture if stakeholders

Figure 7.1. Elements of the School Culture Around Language to Explore

Areas of School Culture to Explore	Questions to Ask When Exploring	Examples of Possible Indications of a Culture Not Focused on Equity Approaches to Language
Mission statement or other values documents from the school, district, and state	Does this document convey value for language diversity and an equity driven approach to language?	Language is focused on appropriateness or standardized language; dominant focus is on English monolingualism.
Behavior or community expectations	Do expectations for community convey a value for language diversity and linguistic fluidity?	There is silence about whether students are welcome to use varied language resources in classrooms.
Curriculum in use at the school site or mandated by the district or state	Does the curriculum adopted or built by teachers contain problematic, limited, or appropriateness-driven approaches to language?	Curriculum itself contains messages that students must use particular language varieties or presents primarily White mainstream forms of English.
Day-to-day instructional practices	Do educators generally attempt language inquiry routines that engage learners in considering language choices and factors that impact these language choices (power, social factors, and communicative goals)?	Instruction can reify language hierarchies or question these hierarchies.
Assessment tools in use at the school site or mandated by the district or state	Do tools guiding classroom assessment center students' purposes and their agency or arbitrary and problematic notions of correctness?	Tools such as rubrics contain language that conveys that some language is incorrect or inappropriate.
Materials used to communicate with caregivers in use at the school site or mandated by the district or state	Do materials sent home with students communicate information in varied languages?	Materials are only available in English.
Professional learning plans in use at the school site or mandated by the district or state	Do professional learning plans allow teachers to collaborate and explore language and content in depth?	Professional learning plans do not address language or do not allow teachers time/ space to collaborate.

Figure 7.1. (continued)

Areas of School Culture to Explore	Questions to Ask When Exploring	Examples of Possible Indications of a Culture Not Focused on Equity Approaches to Language
Visuals	Do artifacts posted on walls throughout the school reflect diverse peoples and language diversity?	Artifacts on walls do not depict any diversity, language or otherwise, or walls are blank.
Extra- and co-curricular spaces	Do the activities outside of classroom instruction allow students opportunities to participate in different language communities?	Activities available for students are limited.

are discouraged, so it is beneficial for the school culture study team to stay positive and fact-driven in their sensemaking process. It is also beneficial to the team to seek feedback from community members on how school culture study team members are perceiving patterns and to ensure that interpretations of data are clear. This often involves connecting with members of the community in ways that invite honest feedback and make all feel welcome. Approaching community members as experts and valued stakeholders, creating multiple channels for feedback (in person, virtual, and written), and establishing a feedback loop that facilitates multiple back-and-forth exchanges will promote positive and truthful interactions around data gathering and interpretation. The final step in the "learning" phase is to present the findings of the school culture study to the community. This could take many forms: a gallery walk that asks all community members to break into groups and read and respond to findings hung up at different stations around a shared room, or a presentation that shares findings and engages the community in discussion and planning. Phase I is ongoing and needs continual refining. So, as the learning phase comes to a close, a critical part of this process is to set new goals for continuous improvement and data collection over time.

At Towering Hill School, Phase I revealed the prevalence of materials at the district and school level that showed a hegemonic and monoglossic approach to language use. Several district-level documents referred to multilingual students entitled to additional English language instruction as "limited English proficient." Observations of faculty meetings showed that this label was taken up widely by educators and administrators who positioned instructional solutions for these learners as about "remediation" of language skills, rather than building on their rich linguistic repertoires. There was even a period during the school day that was referred to as "personalized learning time" that faculty widely considered as remediation time for students designated as English learners. During these time slots, students not designated as English learners often received an advanced phenomenon-based science curriculum or opportunities to select books from the library. Meanwhile, students designated as English learners received instruction focused on English grammar. This realization led the team to examine how the term "limited English proficient" had come to be taken up in informal school communications and the ways instruction was structured and planned. This learning—that deficit labels were shaping instruction—drove the next phase of the school's collective inquiry.

Phase 2: Development

Changing the culture around language requires that schools conceptualize areas for reflection and development that support equitable language instruction. A critical way to engage in this work is through the *creation of professional learning communities* (PLC) dedicated to discussing equitable language teaching. Every educator at a site should be engaged in the development phase and placed in a PLC. Ideally, these groups should meet regularly during the school day. Teachers can choose leadership roles focused on different aspects of language culture and change (e.g., leading activities on language conceptions, organizing discussions around a particular instructional practice). Administrators should set aside time in the school schedule, as well as resources and funding to compensate educators for their time. In these community spaces, we encourage groups to explore teacher beliefs and the connection among teacher beliefs, practices, and principles of instruction. To do this work, we encourage groups to use the Language Mapping activity on page 100, the Reflective Text set activities on page 103–105, as well as group discussion prompts for analyzing teacher language on page 107. These activities often serve to make visible beliefs about language and instructional practices that must be changed as part of moving towards more equitable language teaching. PLCs must be situated in institutions that promote trust among school stakeholders. In communities where there is relational trust, collective inquiry around language can be supported by administrators who encourage a culture of professional reasoning, responsibility, and action around equitable language teaching. Administrators have a central role to play in crafting spaces of trust by modeling productive vulnerability where they share their own current struggles and conceptualize how they can shift aspects of their own leadership to support equity-focused initiatives (Miesner et al., 2022; Khalifa et al., 2016). Administrators and teachers need to work together to reflect on how they wish to address practices that limit equitable language teaching. This phase begins with each group unpacking their own beliefs about language, developing their professional sensemaking (i.e., their pedagogical reasoning, responsibility, and action toward equity), and working collaboratively to conceptualize a way forward that focuses on student and community assets.

Drawing on the learning phase and the equitable language teaching school culture study, school leaders at Towering Hill School as part of Phase 2 asked PLCs at the school to focus on understanding how the term "limited English proficient" negatively shaped instruction for multilingual youth. This focus was introduced by administrators with an acknowledgement that they had not explicitly taken a stance on this language. The Principal explicitly characterized this labeling and framing of multilingual students as "limited" by the district as at odds with the mission and values of Towering Hill School. Moving forward, the school community would work together to avoid this framing while still working within existing district constraints. The principal and the school culture study team then asked each small group to identify ways that this label was shaping their teaching. Then, they proposed concrete ways that the community could address these inequitable language practices. In one of the first meetings of the PLC, one educator reflected: "For me, it's been a real focus on remediation for multilingual kids, I mean the term 'limited' certainly shapes how I think about teaching this group." Others in the group responded with evidence that multilingual students actually were performing better on standardized measures of reading by 4th grade than their monolingual classmates in the district, demonstrating that a focus on remediation seemed problematic. Some small groups began to propose changes to the way they referred to multilingual youth, settling on the term, "emerging bi/multilinguals."

Other small groups questioned ideas about instruction: Were they accelerating the language development of multilingual students by offering the richest and most engaging language learning opportunities they could create? The PLCs at Towering Hill School engaged in language activities geared toward analyzing their own linguistic fluidity such as the Language Mapping activity and Reflective Text Set activities. Afterward, it was not uncommon to hear teachers emphasizing that languages students bring to the classroom were an instructional resource. And educators raised questions about how to make the benefits of multilingualism more visible to students themselves. In the past, comments that students "don't have language" were common in the teachers' room. Now, conversations shifted through use of asset-focused language: "Javier really seems to understand the concept of argumentation and has the language to persuade in Spanish; how can I help him to develop this in English?" Based on ideas of professional sensemaking and with the collaboration and input of the school leadership, teachers at Towering Hill School co-developed a new set of community-building expectations that centered equity in language. They asked staff members to help come up with ideas for how these new expectations could be communicated to students through visual and day-to-day practice routines.

Phase 3: Action

Building towards equitable language teaching requires new structures to support equitable practice. At some school sites, this might involve funding new professional learning that allows educators to acquire additional practices for teaching language in the classroom. At others, setting the agenda for building requires setting aside dedicated time for teachers and administrators to collectively do this work. The building phase follows many of the same processes required for change in Phase 2, such as regular PLC meetings. There are multiple facets to constructing a sturdy space for equitable language teaching. Equitable language teaching practices connect diverse educational stakeholders in their mission, focus, and goals for action. A central element of this phase is using practices that support equity as the focus for all stakeholders. Language-awareness inquiry routines create linguistic connections across classroom topics, subjects, and classrooms. These connections create meaningful and strong relationships between schools, families, and communities (e.g., creating opportunities to solicit linguistic expertise from families or neighborhood groups). When multiple schools in a district embrace values and practices that support linguistic fluidity and varied linguistic resources, this creates sturdy building blocks for advocacy work at the district level (e.g., evident in district-level language policy, professional learning offered district wide, and in curricular decisions made by central office).

This phase of collective inquiry moves beyond deconstruction of the school's existing culture around language towards reimagining and acting on the ways in which language is taught and conceptualized. Consistent with work by Cochran-Smith and Lytle (2021), inquiry, when viewed as a teacher stance or approach to the profession of teaching and schooling, must involve activism. That is, an inquiry stance requires an interrogation of teaching, learning, and schooling so that equity-based changes can be made for teachers, students, and the school culture more broadly. This often involves the collective work of reimagining what can be at a school site—envisioning new curriculum, redesigning professional learning, or instantiating new policies around language use in classrooms.

At Towering Hill School, new instructional practices needed to be built to achieve the faculty's vision for more equitable language teaching. For example, professional learning was particularly useful as it helped teachers to reflect on and share their pedagogical aims in ways that promoted linguistic equity. Professional learning community meetings focused on co-developing language-awareness inquiry routines and using transformative and metalinguistic aims as core principles for guiding instruction. Educators worked together to implement new language-awareness inquiry routine prompts, planning their instruction around transformative and metalinguistic aspects of their content. Once these inquiry routines became embedded in daily instruction, educators posed questions like: "Let's unpack the language in this text—why did the author choose this word? What other language could they use?" Students comfortably used a range of dialects and languages in class discussions. Observations of classrooms showed that teachers asked questions about student ideas and modeled rich and varied language. Teachers also encouraged discussion participation from all students using any language a student chose. Lastly, conversations of content were easily tied back to how language conveys meaning and the idea that all language is situated in systems of power.

At the whole-school level, embracing practices to support linguistic fluidity called for creating access to translation services for caregivers and offering more opportunity to encounter various languages other than English in school settings such as the library and cafeteria. This shift also led to changes in how Towering Hill engaged families. Previously, there had been few opportunities for educators to learn about how language was used in students' homes and community settings. Now, monthly "cafecitos" and family nights that invited faculty at Towering Hill to converse with students' families created an environment for exchanging linguistic knowledge. Towering Hill administrators also led the creation of new documents that embraced more linguistically inclusive labels. While the district still refers to students as "limited English proficient," this label no longer appears in the documents written by Towering Hill School administrators and educators.

All stakeholders at Towering Hill School saw equitable language teaching practices as the touchstone, with teachers honing their craft in this area, and administrators providing increased opportunities for linguistic fluidity to be showcased and promoted. With support from the administration, educators at Towering Hill were given the opportunity to join standing committees in the district that were redesigning instructional guidelines for multilingual youth. Funding provided by the school also gave educators the chance to engage in professional societies at the state level that were engaged in working towards more equitable language teaching models. There is often work to do to transform the linguistic culture at a school site. This work is best done collectively and over time to bring about enduring change.

LEARNED, CHANGED, AND BUILT

Collective inquiry that aims to learn, change, and build a school culture focused on equitable language teaching can support long-lasting change for the school community and beyond. This process is one that requires time and effort, as well as the dedicated involvement of many. But it's also worth the effort. It ensures a more equitable and humanizing learning environment for students who have been marginalized for too long. This welcoming and supportive process can create the potential for language development that is nuanced, supportive, and sets all students up for success and self-empowerment. As this collective inquiry process grows across schools and districts, communities can dismantle problematic language hierarchies on a larger scale. We all must be part of the struggle for justice.

PLANNING FOR ACTION FOR THE COMMUNITY

Tips For Learning, Changing, and Building Linguistic Equity

Learning Phase: *School stakeholders work together to examine current practices through an equitable language teaching school culture study.*

- **Question(s) to ask:** What are the structures (e.g., teams, curricular materials, daily schedules) and processes (ways of interacting) that are currently in place at our school site to teach language? Do these structures and processes promote a culture of equitable language teaching?

THEN

- **Structures:** Create a collaborative team of varied educational stakeholders to conduct the school culture study.
- **Processes:** Collect relevant data, analyze, and examine data using question prompts that address the school culture around language and equity (e.g., Figure 7.1), present findings to the school and community that facilitate honest and constructive back-and-forth exchanges.

Change Phase: *School stakeholders work together to conceptualize areas for growth and set goals that involve reflection as well as personal and professional risk-taking.*

- **Question to ask:** What structures and processes must we leave behind or change to teach language equitably at our school?

THEN

- **Structures:** Create or make use of existing professional learning communities and set aside regular time for the work of these teams.
- **Processes:** Engage in reflective activities on school language beliefs and practices, and the connection between beliefs and practices that support professional sensemaking (e.g., language mapping, reflective text set activities, reflective and reframing discussion prompts, and co-planning prompts for language awareness inquiry routines).

Building Phase: *The school community collaborates to create their vision for equitable language instruction through community action.*

- **Question to ask:** What new structures and processes are needed to teach language equitably at our school?

THEN

- **Structures:** Create new teams (e.g., new professional learning communities, or novel mixed administrator and teacher teams).
- **Processes:** Work in teams to engage in community action, with equitable language instruction being the throughline schoolwide (e.g., language-awareness inquiry routines, teaching and learning activities that support linguistic fluidity).

A VISION FOR EQUITABLE LANGUAGE TEACHING

We end this book where we began: in Ms. Fitz's kindergarten classroom. During Ms. Fitz's science lesson on plant growth and corn, Fiorella, a recent immigrant from Peru, asked about the type of corn under investigation, using words from her native language. Was the corn *"choclo,"* a starchy large kernel corn, or *"maíz,"* a more generic term for corn, commonly sweet corn? In this instructional moment and throughout the school year, Ms. Fitz regularly reflects on how the linguistic diversity in her class creates rich opportunities to explore language. In this case, Fiorella's contributions showcased how language can highlight distinctions between different varieties and characteristics of corn. Drawing from her professional work and learning with colleagues at Towering Hill, Ms. Fitz asked students to consider how this additional language helped enhance their observation skills (e.g., what features of corn were they noticing now: shape, color, size?). We watched as she engaged Fiorella and her peers in language-awareness inquiry routines, and how these back-and-forth exchanges helped the class powerfully harness their entire repertoire of linguistic resources to develop strong observation skills as part of this science lesson. At Towering Hill, all educators, not just Ms. Fitz, are working together to create a school culture where this type of linguistic inquiry is commonplace.

In the adjoining building, two floors up, 6th-graders, as part of their unit on immigration in the United States, work on their own personal language maps that visually display the different language communities they participate in based on their geography, culture, interests, and social and family spaces. A floor above, the 8th-graders explore a series of math lessons focused on understanding and representing visually engagement in STEM fields across sociodemographic groups. And in 8th-grade social studies, these same students examine post-WWII shifts in women's workforce participation. At the center of learning, across these content area classrooms and grades, is question-asking by teachers and students that is metalinguistic (i.e., attends to linguistic features and choices that communicate conceptual understandings) and transformational (i.e., critiques how language functions to preserve or contest power relationships and the role of language for self-expression). A cultural shift towards valuing linguistic pluralism and linguistic flexibility is the work of many and necessitates collective exploration, reflection, and action.

The work of Ms. Fitz and other educators push back against linguicism and reductive practices for teaching language. But it requires both individual and collective effort throughout the school site. To create classrooms where language-awareness inquiry is a central feature of instruction, we must address historical and present manifestations of reductive language teaching in single classrooms as well as the larger culture of a school. We cannot change what we do not yet see. And so this process begins with inquiry—learning about current beliefs and practices around language teaching to support us to change and to build practices that lead to a linguistically just future.

We advocate for whole-school models that support this work and for a culture of equitable language teaching. However, we also recognize that schools can't change overnight and that if we wait for the most fertile space or moment for these changes, we put off acting against the existing systems that marginalize many of our students in schools. We encourage educators to work within their local context, as imperfect as they may be, to join us in building schools that not only teach, but learn, support, grow, and embrace the collective humanity—and complex and nuanced language use—of all children and communities for the purpose of building a more just and equitable tomorrow.

FINAL CLOSING REFLECTION

Consider how you might advocate at your school site to do work toward a school culture focused on equitable language teaching. How might you advocate for a change in this direction as an individual community member? Who would you like to work with to make these changes and how could you see your school culture changing for the better when it comes to language? And, most importantly, what is something you can do starting now to begin to make your school and classroom a more linguistically equitable place?

Glossary

Adaptive teaching: Adjusting instruction to fit the linguistic, cultural, and instructional needs of students. Adaptive teachers anchor teaching in real world learning opportunities; center students' interests and motivations; honor and invite students' cultures, languages, and backgrounds into academic learning; and self-reflect to understand how moment-to-moment instructional moves can impact student learning.

Black English language: A language variation referred to in other sources as "African American English" or "African American Vernacular English" or "Black English." Notably, these different terms have distinct socio-cultural, socio-political, and historical connotations. Black English language refers to a dialect associated with Black communities in the United States.

Discourse: describes a linguistic unit beyond a sentence. Practices to support understanding a discourse include attending to linguistic structures and organization beyond the sentence level (e.g., a cause and effect or problem with a solution text structure).

Equitable instruction: Offering and including different resources in response to diverse student interests, needs, backgrounds and histories. In the context of the U.S. education system that has a history of unequal treatment of students from non-dominant race, ethnic, religious, and linguistic groups, it is an injustice to provide identical resources to all students, because students do not start on equal footing in this historically unjust education system. Equitable instruction, that is, a focus on equity, not equality, centers extending the resources that respond to diverse students needs, wants, and backgrounds to rectify historical inequality.

Inquiry: A process of generating context-specific knowledge, by questioning and exploring assumptions, to create a critical space for reimagining new and more just solutions.

Language-awareness inquiry routines: a content-directed process of question-asking by teachers and students that draws students' attention to the power of language, flexible linguistic choices at their disposal, and their own power of self-expression. These back-and-forth exchanges are driven by prompts that are metalinguistic (i.e., attend to linguistic features such as vocabulary, syntax, and discourse) and transformational (i.e., attend to language that resists and instantiates power and exclusionary forces).

Language hierarchies: Conceptions of language that see some languages as more prestigious than others and thus privilege standardized languages in teaching and learning, at the exclusion of other language varieties.

Languaging: Language used as a tool for participation in social actions.

Linguicism: Discrimination based on one's language, a form of linguistic prejudice.

Linguistic fluidity: a characteristic of a classroom (i.e., a linguistically permeable space) as well as an ability of students and teachers to move seamlessly and consciously between language mastered in different contexts and settings they inhabit in and out of school.

Metalanguage: Language (e.g., terms) that allows one to talk about language and features of language.

Metalinguistic instruction: Pedagogy that explicitly attends to and manipulates features of language use (e.g., vocabulary, syntax, and discourse) and supports reflection on language choices.

Minoritized: Individuals who have been marginalized because of their non-dominant race, ethnicity, religion, language, sexuality, or citizenship. Marginalized students have been disadvantaged by historically oppressive structures and systems. Learners who speak a minortized English, speak a language variation that deviates from standardized English, such as Southern American English.

Monoglossic ideology: The view that English monolingualism is the standard and proficiency in standardized languages should be the overarching goal of instruction.

Professional sensemaking: How educators make sense of their professional practice. This sensemaking, or judgement involves three elements: *pedagogical actions* comprised of intentional and unintentional choices that educators make; *pedagogical reasoning,* which refers to the rationale or reasons for these actions; and, *pedagogical responsibility*, which entails teachers' sense of obligations (moral, ethical, institutional) that frequently undergird reasoning about instruction and actions in the classroom.

Scripts: Language to perform specific patterns, conventions, rules, and ways of disseminating and acting upon information that are set by specific communities.

Syntax: Systematic ways in which words are combined to make sentences and clauses.

Technocratic instruction: Pedagogy where teachers have little discretion in their pedagogical choices, and instead formal standardized systems are in place to routinize instructional practices, materials, and experiences and reduce variation across teachers.

Transformational instruction: Instruction that is grounded in uncovering injustice for the purpose of working toward social transformation.

Translanguaging: Language use where the speaker fluidly moves between two languages in ways consistent with a view of multilingual language resources as integrated.

Vocabulary: Word meanings.

References

Alim, S. (2010). Critical language awareness. In N. H. Hornberger & S. L. McKay (Eds.), *Sociolinguistics and language education* (pp. 205–231). Multilingual Matters.

Alim, H. S., Rickford, J. R., & Ball, A. F. (2016). *Raciolinguistics: How language shapes our ideas about race.* Oxford University Press.

Bailey, A. L. (2007). *The language demands of school.* Yale University Press.

Baker-Bell, A. (2017). I can switch my language, but I can't switch my skin: What teachers must understand about linguistic racism. In E. Moore, A. Michael Jr., & M. W. Penick-Parks (Eds.), *The guide for White women who teach Black boys* (pp. 97–107). Corwin Press.

Baker-Bell, A. (2020a). Dismantling anti-black linguistic racism in English language arts classrooms. *Theory Into Practice, 59*(1).

Baker-Bell, A. (2020b). *Linguistic justice: Black language, literacy, identity, and pedagogy.* Routledge.

Bakhtin, M. M. (1981). *The dialogic imagination: Four essays* (M. Holquist, Ed.). University of Texas Press.

Baumann, J. F., Kame'enui, E. J., & Ash, G. (2003). Research on vocabulary instruction: Voltaire redux. In J. Flood, D. Lapp, J. R. Squire, & J. Jensen (Eds.), *Handbook of research on teaching the English language arts* (2nd ed., pp. 752–785). Erlbaum.

Beck, I. L., McKeown, M. G., & Kucan, L. (2013). *Bringing words to life: Robust vocabulary instruction* (2nd ed.). Guilford Press.

Berman, R. A., & Ravid, D. (2009). Becoming a literate language user: Oral and written text construction across adolescence. In D. R. Olson & N. Torrance (Eds.), *Cambridge handbook of literacy* (pp. 92–111). Cambridge University Press.

Berninger, V. W., Nagy, W., & Beers, S. (2010). Child writers' construction and reconstruction of single sentences and construction of multi-sentence texts: Contributions of syntax and transcription to translation. *Reading and Writing, 24*, 151–182. https://doi.org/10.1007/s11145-010-9262-y

Blum-Kulka, S. (2008). Language, communication and literacy: Major steps in the development of literate discourse. In P. Klein & Y. Yablon (Eds.), *From research to practice in early education* (pp. 117–154). Israeli Academy of Science.

Bonilla-Silva, E. (2015). More than prejudice: Restatement, reflections, and new directions in Critical Race Theory. *Sociology of Race and Ethnicity, 1*(1), 73–87.

Bryk, A. S., Gomez, L. M., Grunow, A., & LeMahieu, P. (2015). *Learning to improve: How America's schools can get better at getting better.* Harvard Education Press.

Buehl, D. (2011). *Developing readers in the academic disciplines*. International Reading Association.

Chen, G., Marshall, S., & Horn, I. (2020). "How do I choose?": Mathematics teachers' sensemaking about pedagogical responsibility. *Pedagogy, Culture and Society*, 1–18.

Chetty, R., Friedman, J. N., & Rockoff, J. E. (2014). Measuring the impacts of teachers II: Teacher value-added and student outcomes in adulthood. *The American Economic Review, 104*(9), 2633–2679. http://www.jstor.org/stable/43495328

Coates, T.-N. (October 4, 2017). Civil-rights protests have never been popular: Activists can't persuade their contemporaries—they're aiming at the next generation. *The Atlantic*.

Cochran-Smith, M., & Lytle, S. (2009). *Inquiry as stance: Practitioner research for the next generation*. Teachers College Press.

Cochran-Smith, M., & Lytle, S. L. (2021). Inquiry in the age of data: A commentary. *Teaching Education, 32*(1), 99–99. https://doi.org/10.1080/10476210.2020.1868142

Corson, D. (1997). The learning and use of academic English words. *Language Learning, 47*(4), 671–718.

Crawford, J. (2000). *At war with diversity: US language policy in an age of anxiety* (Vol. 25). Multilingual Matters.

Creswell, J. W. (2018). *Qualitative inquiry and research design: Choosing among five approaches* (4th ed.). Sage Publications, Inc.

Darling-Hammond, L., Wei, R. C., Andree, A., Richardson, N., & Orphanos, S. (2009). State of the profession: Study measures status of professional development. *Journal of Staff Development, 30*(2), 42–50.

de los Ríos, C. V., Martinez, D. C., Musser, A. D., Canady, A., Camangian, P., & Quijada, P. D. (2019). Upending colonial practices: Toward repairing harm in English Education. *Theory Into Practice, 58*(4), 359–367.

Deroo, M. R., & Ponzio, C. M. (2021). Fostering pre-service teachers' critical multilingual language awareness: Use of multimodal compositions to confront hegemonic language ideologies. *Journal of Language, Identity & Education*, 1–17.

Diaz, B. (1963). *The conquest of new Spain*. The Penguin Group. New York, NY.

Dobbs, C. L., Ippolito, J., & Charner-Laird, M. (2017). *Investigating disciplinary literacy: A framework for collaborative professional learning*. Harvard Education Press.

Duff, P. A. (2010). Language socialization into academic discourse communities. *Annual Review of Applied Linguistics, 30*, 169–192.

Duncan, A. F. (2005). *Honey baby sugar child*. Simon & Schuster Books for Young Readers.

Edmonson, A. C. (2018). *The fearless organization: Creating psychological safety in the workplace for learning, innovation and growth*. Wiley.

Elleman, A. M., Lindo, E. J., Morphy, P., & Compton, D. L. (2009). The impact of vocabulary instruction on passage-level comprehension of school-age children: A meta-analysis.

Elmore, R. F. (1996). Commentary: School reform, teaching and learning. *Journal of Education Policy, 11*(4), 499–504.

Enderle, P., Dentzau, M., Roseler, K., Southerland, S., Granger, E., Hughes, R., Golden, B., & Saka, Y. (2014). Examining the Influence of RETs on science teacher beliefs and practice. *Science Education, 98*(6), 1077–1108.

Fitzgerald, J., Elmore, J., Relyea, J. E., & Stenner, A. J. (2020). Domain-specific academic vocabulary network development in elementary grades core disciplinary textbooks. *Journal of Educational Psychology, 112*(5), 855–879. https://doi.org/10.1037/edu0000386

Flanigan, K., & Greenwood, S. C. (2007). Effective content vocabulary instruction in the middle: Matching students, purposes, words, and strategies. *Journal of Adolescent & Adult Literacy, 51*(3), 226–238.

Frost, R., Untermeyer, L., & Frost, R. (1991). *The road not taken: A selection of Robert Frost's poems*. H. Holt and Co.

Fullan, M. (2001). *Leading in a culture of change*. Jossey-Bass.

García, O. (1991). *Bilingual education: Focus shift in honor of Joshua A. Fishman on the occasion of his 65th birthday*. John Benjamins Publishing Company.

García, O., & Wei, Li. (2014). *Translanguaging: Implications for language, bilingualism and education*. Palgrave Pivot.

Gee, J. P. (1996). *Social linguistics and literacies: Ideology in discourse*. Taylor and Francis.

Gee, J. P. (2012). *Situated language and learning: A critique of traditional schooling*. Taylor and Francis.

Gehlbach, H., Brinkworth, M. E., & Harris, A. D. (2012). Changes in teacher–student relationships. *British Journal of Educational Psychology, 82*, 690–704. http://dx.doi.org/10.1111/j.2044-8279.2011.02058.x

Gist, C. D. (2017). Voices of aspiring teachers of color: Unraveling the double bind in teacher education. *Urban Education, 52*(8), 927–956. https://doi.org/10/1177/004208591562339

Gottlieb, M., & Ernst-Slavit, G. (2014). *Academic language in diverse classrooms: Definitions and contexts*. Corwin Press.

Greenfield, E. (2016). *Honey, I love*. HarperCollins.

Gutiérrez, K. D., Morales, P. Z., & Martinez, D. C. (2009). Re-mediating literacy: Culture, difference, and learning for students from nondominant communities. *Review of Research in Education, 33*(1), 212–245.

Halliday, M. A. K., & Hasan, R. (1990). *Language, context, and text: Aspects of language in a social-semiotic perspective*. Oxford University Press.

Hallinger, P., & Heck, R. H. (2011). Collaborative leadership and school improvement: Understanding the impact on school capacity and student learning. In T. Townsend & J. Macbeath (Eds.), *International handbook of leadership for learning* (pp. 469–485). Springer.

Hanno, E. C. (2022). Immediate changes, trade-offs, and fade-out in high-quality teacher practices during coaching. *Educational Researcher, 51*(3), 173–185.

Heck, R. H., & Marcoulides, G. A. (1996). School culture and performance: Testing the invariance of an organizational model. *School Effectiveness and School Improvement, 7*(1), 76–96.

Heineke, A., & Neugebauer, S. R. (2018). The complexity of language and learning: Deconstructing teachers' conceptions of academic language. *Issues in Teacher Education, 27*(3), 73–89.

Hill, H. C. (2004). Professional development standards and practices in elementary school mathematics. *Elementary School Journal, 104*(3), 215–231.

Holler, J., Kendrick, K. H., & Levinson, S. C. (2018). Processing language in face-to-face conversation: Questions with gestures get faster responses.

Psychonomic Bulletin & Review, 25(5), 1900–1908. https://doi.org/10.3758/s13423-017-1363-z

Holt California life science. (2007). Holt, Rinehart, and Winston.

hooks, b. (2017). *Homemade love.* Jump at the Sun.

Hopkins, M., Spillane, J. P., Jakopovic, P., & Heaton, R. M. (2013). Infrastructure redesign and instructional reform in mathematics: Formal structure and teacher leadership. *Elementary School Journal, 114*(2), 200–224.

Horn, I. S. & Campbell, S. S. (2015). Developing pedagogical judgment in novice teachers: Mediated field experience as a pedagogy for teacher education. *Pedagogies: An International Journal, 10*(2), 149–176.

Hoy, W. K. (1990). Organizational climate and culture: A conceptual analysis of the school workplace. *Journal of Educational and Psychological Consultation, 1*(2): 149–168.

Hyland, K. (2004). *Genre and second language writing.* The University of Michigan Press.

Ishimaru, A. M., Barajas-López, F., Sun, M., Scarlett, K., & Anderson, E. (2022). Transforming the role of RPPs in remaking educational systems. *Educational Researcher.* Advance online publication. https://doi.org/10.3102/0013189X221098077

Janks, H. (2000). Domination, access, diversity and design: A synthesis for critical literacy education. *Educational Review, 52*(2), 175–186.

Jones, B. F, Palincsar, A. S., Ogle, D. S., & Carr, E. G. (Eds.). (1987). *Strategic teaching and learning: Cognitive instruction in the content areas.* Association for Supervision and Curriculum Development.

Kasmer, L. A., & Kim, O. (2012). The nature of student predictions and learning opportunities in middle school algebra. *Educational Studies in Mathematics, 79*(2), 175–191. http://dx.doi.org/10.1007/s10649-011-9336-z

Kendi, I. X. (2019). *How to be an antiracist.* One World Publishers.

Kennedy, M. M. (2016). How does professional development improve teaching? *Review of Educational Research, 86*, 945–980.

Kinloch, V., Penn, C., & Burkhard, T. (2020). Black lives matter: Storying, identities, and counternarratives. *Journal of Literacy Research, 52*(4), 382–405. https://doi.org/10.1177/1086296X20966372

Khalifa, M. A., Gooden, M. A., & Davis, J. E. (2016). Culturally responsive school leadership: A synthesis of the literature. *Review of Educational Research, 86*(4), pp. 1272–1311. doi: 10.3102/0034654316630383

Kucan, L. & Palincsar, A. S. (2013). *Comprehension instruction through text-based discussion.* Newark, DE: International Reading Association.

Kumashiro, K. K. (2000). Toward a theory of anti-oppressive education. *Review of Educational Research, 70*(1), 25–53.

Kumashiro, K. K. (2001). "Posts" perspectives on anti-oppressive education in social studies, English, mathematics, and science classrooms. *Educational Researcher, 30*(3), 3–12.

Kumashiro, K. K. (2015). *Against common sense: Teaching and learning toward social justice.* Routledge.

Ladson-Billings, G. (2006). From the achievement gap to the education debt: Understanding achievement in U.S. Schools. *Educational Researcher, 35*(7), 3–12.

Lampert, M., Franke, M., Kazemi, E., Ghousseini, H., Turrou, A., Beasley, H., & Crowe, K. (2013). Keeping it complex: Using rehearsals to support novice teacher learning of ambitious teaching. *Journal of Teacher Education, 64*, 226–243.

Lee, C. D. (2006). "Every good-bye ain't gone": Analyzing the cultural underpinnings of classroom talk. *International Journal of Qualitative Studies in Education, 19*, 305–327.

Lee, C. D. 2007. *Culture, literacy, and learning*. Teachers College Press.

Lemke, J. L. (2002). Language development and identity: Multiple timescales in the social ecology of learning. In C. Kramsch (Ed.), *Language acquisition and language socialization* (pp. 68–87). Continuum.

Lesaux, N. K., Kieffer, M. J., Faller, E. S., & Kelley, J. G. (2010). The effectiveness and ease of implementation of an academic vocabulary intervention for linguistically diverse students in urban middle schools. *Reading Research Quarterly, 45*(2), 196–228.

Lesaux, N. K., Phillip Galloway, E., & Marietta, S. H. (2016). *Teaching advanced literacy skills: A guide for leaders in linguistically diverse schools*. The Guilford Press.

Lewis, A. E., & Diamond, J. B. (2015). *Despite the best intentions: How racial inequality thrives in good schools*. Oxford University Press.

Love, B. L. (2019). *We want to do more than survive: Abolitionist teaching and the pursuit of educational freedom*. Beacon Press.

Lowry, L. (1989). *Number the stars*. Houghton Mifflin.

Lynch, J. (2017). Short-term professional learning that focuses on beliefs and practice: Improvements in preschool teachers' ongoing literacy practice. *Journal of Early Childhood Teacher Education, 38*(2), 164–181.

Martínez, R. A., & Mejía, A. F. (2020). Looking closely and listening carefully: A sociocultural approach to understanding the complexity of Latina/o/x students' everyday language. *Theory Into Practice, 59*(1), 53–63.

McClain, J. B., Harmon, M., & Phillips Galloway, E. (2021). Eliminating prerequisites for personhood: A framework for enacting antiracist language instruction. *Language Arts, 99*(1), 25–36.

Miesner, H., Blair, E., Packard, C., Velazquez, M., Macgregor, L., & Grodsky, E. (2022). Collaborating in context: Relational trust and collaborative formats at eight elementary schools. *Teaching and Teacher Education, 115*. https://doi.org/10.1016/j.tate.2022.103729

Milner, H. R. (2007a). Preservice teachers' learning about cultural and racial diversity: Implications for urban education. *Urban Education, 41*(4), 343–375.

Milner, H. R. (2007b). Race, culture, and researcher positionality: Working through dangers seen, unseen, and unforeseen. *Educational Researcher, 36*(7), 388–400.

Milner, H. R. (2017). *Race to improve teacher education: Building awareness for instructional practice*. American Federation of Teachers. https://www.aft.org/ae/fall2019/milner

Moje, E. B. (2015). Doing and teaching disciplinary literacy with adolescent learners: A social and cultural enterprise. *Harvard Educational Review, 85*, 254–278.

Moore-Johnson, S. (2019). *Where teachers thrive: Organizing schools for success*. Harvard Education Press.

Muhammad, G. (2020). *Cultivating genius: An equity framework for culturally and historically responsive literacy*. Scholastic.

Nagy, W., & Townsend, D. (2012). Words as tools: Learning academic vocabulary as language acquisition. *Reading Research Quarterly*, *47*(1), 91–108.

National Governors Association Center for Best Practices & Council of Chief State School Officers. (2010). Common core state standards for English language arts and literacy in history/social studies, science, and technical subjects. Authors.

National Institute of Child Health and Human Development (NICHD). (2000). Report of the National Reading Panel. Teaching children to read: An evidence-based assessment of the scientific research literature on reading and its implications for reading instruction (NIH Publication No. 00-4769). U.S. Government Printing Office.

Neugebauer, S. R., & Heineke. A. J. (2020a). Teachers' understandings of academic language: Assessing academic language definitions, motivations, and values of teachers. *Teacher Education Quarterly, 46*, 1–25.

Neugebauer, S. R., & Heineke, A. J. (2020b). Unpacking K–12 teachers' understandings of academic language. *Teacher Education Quarterly*, *47*(2), 158–182.

Opfer, V. D., & Pedder, D. (2011). Conceptualizing teacher professional learning. *Review of Educational Research, 81*, 376–407.

Ouellette, G. P. (2006). What's meaning got to do with it: The role of vocabulary in word reading and reading comprehension. *Journal of Educational Psychology, 98*(3), 554–566.

Paris, D. (2012). Culturally sustaining pedagogy: A needed change in stance, terminology, and practice. *Educational Researcher, 41*, 93–97. https://doi.org/10.3102/00131 89X12441244

Paris, D. (2016). "It was a Black city": African American language in California's changing urban schools and communities. In H. Samy Alim, John R. Rickford & Arnetha F. Ball (Eds.), *Raciolinguistics: How language shapes our ideas about race* (pp. 241–254). Oxford University Press.

Paris, D., & Alim, H. S. (2014). What are we seeking to sustain through culturally sustaining pedagogy? A loving critique forward. *Harvard Educational Review, 84*(1), 85–100.

Paris, D., & Alim, H. S. (Eds.). (2017). *Culturally sustaining pedagogies: Teaching and learning for justice in a changing world*. Teachers College Press.

Parsons, S. A., Vaughn, M., Scales, R. Q., Gallagher, M. A., Parsons, A. W., Davis, S. G., Pierczynski, M., & Allen, M. (2018). Teachers' instructional adaptations: A research synthesis. *Review of Educational Research, 88*(2), 205–242.

Patel, L. (2019). Fugitive practices: Learning in a settler colony. *Educational Studies*, *55*(3), 253–261.

Pennycook, A. (2001/2021). *Critical applied linguistics: A critical re-introduction*. Routledge.

Philip, T., Souto-Manning, M., Anderson, L., Horn, I., Andrews, D. J. C., Stillman, J., & Varghese, M. (2019). Making justice peripheral by constructing practice as "core": How the increasing prominence of core practices challenges teacher education. *Journal of Teacher Education*, *70*(3), 251–264. https://doi.org/10.1177/0022487118798324

Phillips Galloway, E., Stude, J., & Uccelli, P. (2015). Adolescents' metalinguistic reflections on the academic register in speech and writing. *Linguistics and Education, 31*, 221–237. http://dx.doi.org/10.1016/j.linged.2014.10.006

Phillips Galloway, E., Meston, H., & Dobbs, C. (2022). Linguistic cartography: Language mapping as a practice for understanding our multilingual students and our own language repertoires. *Journal of Language, Education, & Identity* (online ahead of print).

Phillips Galloway, E. & Uccelli, P. (2019). Beyond reading comprehension: Exploring the additional contribution of academic language skills to early adolescents' source-based writing. *Reading and Writing: An Interdisciplinary Journal, 32*(3), 729–759.

Phillipson, R., & Skutnabb-Kangas, T. (1986). *Linguicism rules in education*, Parts 1–3. Roskilde University Centre, Institute VI.

Roorda, D., Koomen, H., Split, J. L., & Oort, F. J. (2011). The influence of affective teacher–student relationships on students' school engagement and achievement: A meta-analytic approach. *Review of Educational Research, 81*, 493–529.

Schleppegrell, M. J. (2004). *The language of schooling: A functional linguistics perspective*. Erlbaum.

Shanahan, T., & Shanahan, C. (2008). Teaching disciplinary literacy to adolescents: Rethinking content-area literacy. *Harvard Educational Review, 78*(1), 40–59. https://doi.org/10.17763/haer.78.1.v62444321p602101

Skrla, L., Scheurich, J. J., Garcia, J., & Nolly, G. (2004). Equity audits: A practical leadership tool for developing equitable and excellent Schools. *Educational Administration Quarterly, 40*(1), 133–161. https://doi.org/10.1177/0013161X03259148

Skutnabb-Kangas, T. (2015). Linguicism. In C. Chappelle (Ed.), *The encyclopedia of applied linguistics* (pp. 1–6). Wiley-Blackwell.

Snell, E. K., Hindman, A. H., & Wasik, B. A. (2015). How can book reading close the word gap? Five key practices from research. *The Reading Teacher, 68*(7), 560–571. https://doi.org/10.1002/trtr.1347

Snow, C. E., & Kim, Y.-S. (2007). Large problem spaces: The challenge of vocabulary for English language learners. In R. K. Wagner, A. E. Muse, & K. R. Tannenbaum (Eds.), *Vocabulary acquisition: Implications for reading comprehension* (pp. 123–139). Guilford Press.

Snow, C. E., Lawrence, J., & White, C. (2009). Generating knowledge of academic language among urban middle school students. *Journal of Research on Educational Effectiveness, 2*(4), 325–344.

Snow, C. E., & Uccelli, P. (2009). The challenge of academic language. In D. R. Olson & N. Torrance (Eds.), *The Cambridge handbook of literacy* (pp. 112–133). Cambridge University Press.

Solórzano, D. G., & Yosso, T. J. (2001). Critical race and latCrit theory and method: Counter-storytelling. *International Journal of Qualitative Studies in Education, 14*, 37–41.

Souto-Manning, M. (2021). On the abolition of belonging as property: Toward justice for immigrant children of color. *Urban Education*, 1–26. https://doi.org/00420859211017967

Stahl, S. A., & Fairbanks, M. M. (1986). The effects of vocabulary instruction: A model-based meta-analysis. *Review of Educational Research, 56*(1), 72–110. https://doi.org/10.3102/00346543056001072

Star, J. R., Rittle-Johnson, B., & Durkin, K. (2016). Comparison and explanation of multiple strategies: One example of a small step forward for improving mathematics education. *Policy Insights from the Behavioral and Brain Sciences, 3*(2), 151–159. https://doi.org/10.1177/2372732216655543

Starkey, M. G. (2020). *Snakes for kids: A junior scientist's guide to venom, scales, and life in the wild.* Rockridge Press.

Steinbeck, J. (1937). *Of mice and men.* Penguin Classics.

Swain, M. (2006). Languaging, agency and collaboration in advanced second language learning. In H. Byrnes (Ed.), *Advanced language learning: The contributions of Halliday and Vygotsky* (pp. 95–108). Continuum.

Swain, M. (2010). "Talking-it-through": Languaging as a source of learning. In R. Batstone (Ed.), *Sociocognitive perspectives on second language learning and use* (pp. 112–129). Oxford University Press.

Swain, M., & Lapkin, S. (1998). Interaction and second language learning: Two adolescent French immersion students working together. *Modern Language Journal, 82*, 320–337.

Taylor, M. D. (1976). *Roll of thunder, hear my cry.* Puffin.

Tiilikainen, M., Toom, A., Lepola, J., & Husu, J. (2019). Reconstructing choice, reason and disposition in teachers' practical theories of teaching (PTs). *Teaching and Teacher Education, 79*, 124–136.

Townsend, D. R., & Lapp, D. (2010). Academic language, discourse communities and technology: Building students' linguistic resources. *Teacher Education Quarterly, Special Online Edition.* Retrieved from http://teqjournal.org/townsend_lapp.html

Uccelli, P., Barr, C., Dobbs, C., Phillips Galloway, E., Meneses, A., & Sánchez, E. (2015). Core academic language skills: An expanded operational construct and a novel instrument to chart school-relevant language proficiency in preadolescent and adolescent learners. *Applied Psycholinguistics, 36*(5), 1077–1109. https://doi.org/10.1017/S014271641400006X

Uccelli, P., Dobbs, C. L., & Scott, J. (2013). Mastering academic language organization and stance in the persuasive writing of high school students. *Written Communication, 30*, 36–62.

Uccelli, P., & Phillips Galloway, E. (2017). Academic language across content areas: Lessons from an innovative assessment and from students' reflections about language. *Journal of Adolescent & Adult Literacy, 60*, 395–404. https://doi.org/10.1002/jaal.553

Uccelli, P., Phillips Galloway, E., Aguilar, G., & Allen, M. (2020). Amplifying and affirming students' voices through CALS-informed instruction. *Theory Into Practice, 59* (1), 75–88. https://doi.org/10.1080/00405841.2019.1665413

Valdés, G. (2004). Between support and marginalisation: The development of academic language in linguistic minority children. *International Journal of Bilingual Education and Bilingualism, 7*, 102–132.

Valenzuela, E. (2005). *L2 ultimate attainment and the syntax-discourse interface: The acquisition of topic constructions in non-native Spanish and English.* Ph.D. dissertation, McGill University.

van Es, E. A., & Sherin, M. G. (2008). Mathematics teachers "learning to notice" in the context of a video club. *Teaching and Teacher Education, 24*, 244–276.

Vedder-Weiss, D., Ehrenfeld, N., Ram-Menashe, M., & Pollak, I. (2018). Productive framing of pedagogical failure: How teacher framings can facilitate or impede learning from problems of practice. *Thinking Skills and Creativity, 30*, 31–41.

Wineburg, S., Martin, D., & Monte-Sano, C. (2012). *Reading like a historian: Teaching literacy in middle and high school history classrooms*. Teachers College Press.

Wynter-Hoyte, K., & Smith, M. (2020). "Hey, Black child. Do you know who you are?" Using African diaspora literacy to humanize blackness in early childhood education. *Journal of Literacy Research, 52*(4), 406–431. https://doi.org/10.1177/1086296X20967393

Zwiers, J. (2013). *Building academic language: Essential practices for content classrooms, grades 5–12*. John Wiley & Sons.

Zwiers, J., & Hamerla, S. (2018). *The K–3 guide to academic conversations: Practices, scaffolds and activities*. Corwin Press.

Index

About the Authors

Dr. Sabina Neugebauer is an associate professor of literacy in the College of Education at Temple University. Dr. Neugebauer's research focuses on the language and literacy development of students in urban elementary and middle schools. Her work explores two aspects of efficacious reading: vocabulary and reading motivation. She investigates these two facets of reading at three complementary levels of analysis (individual, classroom, and school context) to more comprehensively identify ways to support students in achieving equitable educational outcomes. Her scholarship identifies prominent sources of reading differences between individuals, evaluates classroom practices that empower student success, and designs assessments to help schools increase their use of evidence-based programs schoolwide. She has served as a reading interventionist and also collaborated with urban schools in the United States and in Latin America to develop multilingual, multi-tiered, and digital reading programs. Dr. Neugebauer is the recipient of the Outstanding Early Career Scholar Award from AERA's Division C, Learning and Instruction, and the International Literacy Association's Elva Knight award. Her research has been supported by the Institute of Education Sciences, the Spencer Foundation, and the U.S. Department of Education to improve the schooling experiences of multilingual students. She is also a co-author of *Interventions for Reading Problems: Designing and Evaluating Effective Strategies*, published by Guilford Press and *Indigenous Knowledge and Education: Sites of Struggle, Strength and Survivance,* published by Harvard Educational Publishing Group.

Emily Phillips Galloway is an assistant professor at Vanderbilt University's Peabody School of Education. Rooted in her experiences as a former middle school reading specialist, Phillips Galloway's quantitative and qualitative research explores the relationships between school-relevant language development and language expression and comprehension during middle childhood with a particular focus on linguistically and culturally minoritized learners. Her quantitative studies demonstrate links between school-relevant language and reading and writing performances, revealing the importance of attending to language beyond the word-level in order to support the literacy development of middle school students. Phillips Galloway's qualitative work situated in classrooms demonstrates the potential for developing these school-relevant language skills through talk that builds on students' out-of-school language resources (dialectal and additional languages) and that fosters agency in linguistic choice-making. With the goal of advancing anti-racist pedagogy, her work aims to positions school-relevant language as a semiotic resource for critically examining inequality, envisioning change, fostering learner agency, and nurturing minoritized learners' socio-emotional, professional, and political aspirations. With a commitment to advancing research-practice partnerships, she has also worked with teachers, school leaders, and administrators in two of the largest urban districts in the United States. The fundamentals and lessons learned from this work are featured in a recent book entitled, *Advanced Literacy Instruction in Linguistically Diverse Settings: A Guide for School Leaders* (2016), co-authored with Nonie Lesaux and Sky Marietta. This book offers a blueprint for leading literacy instruction that supports all learners. She is a recipient of the AERA-SRCD Early Career Fellowship in Middle Childhood Education and Development (2019–2021).

Dr. Christina L. Dobbs is an assistant professor and director of the English Education program at Boston University Wheelock College of Education and Human Development. Her research interests include academic language development, the argumentative writing of students, and professional development for secondary content teachers. Her work has been published in the *Journal of Adolescent and Adult Literacy, Reading Research Quarterly, Professional Development in Education,* and the *Journal of School Leadership*. She is the author of several books, including *Investigating Disciplinary Literacy* (2017) and *Disciplinary Literacy Inquiry & Instruction* (2019). She is a former high school teacher in Houston, Texas, as well as a literacy coach and reading specialist.